T0096728

LIFE LESSONS ON FRIENDSHIP

LIFE LESSONS
ON FRIENDSHIP

13 honest tales of
the most important
relationships of our lives

Edited by Mandie Gower

PENGUIN LIFE

AN IMPRINT OF

PENGUIN BOOKS

PENGUIN LIFE

UK | USA | Canada | Ireland | Australia
India | New Zealand | South Africa

Penguin Life is part of the Penguin Random House group of companies
whose addresses can be found at global.penguinrandomhouse.com.

First published 2021
001

Set in 10.25/18pt Futura Std
Typeset by Jouve (UK), Milton Keynes
Printed and bound in Great Britain by Clays Ltd, Elcograf S.p.A.

A CIP catalogue record for this book is available from the British Library

ISBN: 978-0-241-38497-8

www.greenpenguin.co.uk

CONTENTS

INTRODUCTION

What does it mean to be a good friend? That, in essence, is the question we posed to the fifteen inspiring women who have contributed to this book.

For if the last few years have shown us anything, it's that friendship is a powerful force that can achieve extraordinary things, from global campaigns sparked by sisterhood to game-changing businesses built on college bonds. And it was on the principle of friendship that *Stylist* was launched back in 2009, too, promising to unite and empower women, sharing each other's experiences and celebrating their successes.

So it seemed fitting that we follow our hugely successful *Life Lessons from Remarkable Women* (2018) and *Beauty Reimagined* (2019), by asking fifteen of our favourite women, among them author Candice Brathwaite, broadcaster Dame Jenni Murray, influencer Megan Jayne Crabbe and MP Alison McGovern, to explore what friendship means today.

Moving, heart-warming and occasionally messy, their lessons are a valuable reminder that friendships are as diverse as the women who form them. That there is no one way to be a good friend, but that a great one really *can* change your life . . .

— Lisa Smosarski, Editor-in-chief, *Stylist*

MEGAN JAYNE CRABBE

A love letter to platonic soulmates

Megan Jayne Crabbe or – as her million-strong Instagram followers know her, @Bodyposipanda – is a body positivity campaigner and author. An eating disorder recovery advocate, Megan's message is unapologetically feminist, and her empowering words and joyful dancing videos have been shared around the world. She followed her bestselling book Body Positive Power *with a UK tour of her live show,* Never Say Diet Club, *and starred in Little Mix's music video,* Strip. *Megan is also a carer to her sister Gemma, who has cerebral palsy.*

I went for a walk one morning at the start of the year. The sky was glaring white and a hint of green was just starting to bravely show itself on the branches. An icy breeze brushed the few slivers of skin unprotected by woolly layers, a visceral reminder of how raw everything still felt. It must have been about three weeks after . . .

I'd been swimming in feelings since that day – drowning some days, fiercely thrashing my way to the surface on others, defiantly refusing to be dragged under. But that morning, I couldn't keep the wave from swelling up. My legs kept moving, through overhanging trees and down a muddy slope, until eventually, I had to stop. I stood in the middle of a clearing, pulled out my phone and started typing, my thoughts and emotions spilling out through my fingertips. Here, at twenty-six years old, I was exactly where I'd never expected to be – suddenly single after 2,720 days of being someone's girlfriend.

Straight after my break-up, my best friends showed up for me in ways that I didn't even know were possible. One began the process of packing up her life and moving in with me so that the house I was suddenly alone in wouldn't feel so cold and empty. One started checking in every day and creating space for me to pour out every passing emotion, which she would then hold and gently tilt towards the light so that I could see another way through it. One distracted me with graphic imaginary future dates featuring all the wild and experimental sex I was soon to be having. One agreed to run away with me to somewhere hot as soon as reality started feeling like too much. And another started holding my hand in public when I told her how much I missed being held.

I'd spent a lot of the previous eight years settling into the idea that the person I was with was probably my soulmate. If you're hearing a touch of doubt in the way I've worded that, you'd be absolutely correct; I never stopped being doubtful about whether we were soulmates. But I roughly nestled myself into the word, anyway, like a new jumper that you know looks good, even though it's quietly scratching at you from the inside.

To be honest, I wasn't sure I believed in soulmates when I met him. Rationally, the odds of finding one person out of billions who fits every one of your facets always seemed pretty unlikely to me. The chances that I could have found that person in a club on a local night out when I was eighteen, where I'd spent most of the evening pretending to be a Disney princess with my best friend and telling men that my name was Pocahontas . . . also somewhat unlikely.

But there I'd been, convincing myself to believe in a concept that a younger version of me had spent years dreaming about. I blame these fantasies at least a little bit on Melissa Joan Hart throwing down that jagged stone heart in the series finale of *Sabrina the Teenage Witch*, and it being met, inevitably, by Harvey's matching half. Every line and crack filled perfectly by the other's piece – *meant to be*. Of course I wanted that, too – who the hell wouldn't? Riding off into the sunset on the back of my soulmate's motorbike wouldn't have gone amiss either. So when someone came along who told me that's what we were, I was ready to chip away at my stone to make the shape fit.

And yet there were lots of small cracks at the start that we never really filled. Ultimately, trying to reach across the gaps was doing us both more harm than good, and it was kinder to stop reaching. In a lot of ways, leaving that relationship felt like growing back the parts I'd roughly chiselled off. Letting my opinions be less filtered. Reclaiming my time to spend how I wanted. Putting my energy back into myself. Stretching out into old passions

I'd let go of and leaping into new goals I'd never let myself say out loud.

During those early weeks I felt new dimensions growing nearly every day, a lot of them spiky and unrefined and unpretty. But the people who still recognized me, even when I didn't know myself, were my friends. I think part of me always knew that they'd be there long after him, so I'd stayed close with them throughout my relationship, never letting them go far. One morning my flatmate emerged from her room and announced that we should go for a night out in a town that was a four-hour drive away. We could play mini-golf when we got there, she said, as if mini-golf were a phenomenon that didn't exist closer to home. I said yes immediately. Not for the golf or the clubbing, but because long drives with her always felt like going exactly where I was supposed to go. Nobody else knows every word to the emo anthems of our teenage years like she does.

Singing my throat raw while afternoon sun streamed through the car window and into our eyes felt like the most clearly another person has ever seen me.

Pouring myself into my relationships with my friends, I slowly realized, gave me nearly every kind of connection I'd been missing over those years. They listened and actually heard me. They helped me paint what I wanted my world to look like and cheered when there was progress. They made me remember how it felt to cackle until black streaks of mascara ran down my cheeks and strangers stared, confused by our shrieks.

In short, my friends threw down their metaphorical soul stones and – no, unlike Sabrina's happily ever after, they didn't fit completely with mine. Instead, our jutting, uneven edges splayed out in parallel directions, creating a pattern more extraordinary than her perfect heart. A mosaic too multidimensional

POURING MYSELF INTO MY RELATIONSHIPS WITH MY FRIENDS, I SLOWLY REALIZED, GAVE ME NEARLY EVERY KIND OF CONNECTION I'D BEEN MISSING OVER THOSE YEARS. THEY LISTENED AND ACTUALLY HEARD ME. THEY HELPED ME PAINT WHAT I WANTED MY WORLD TO LOOK LIKE AND CHEERED WHEN THERE WAS PROGRESS.

to be one coherent shape, and even more beautiful that way.

What are the chances, I wondered during those first few weeks of being single, that a group of girls from a tiny seaside town in Essex, raised in wildly different ways and set for paths in opposite directions, would wind up bound back together the way we are? A group of women I've known since I was eleven years old, back when we first started holding hands with boys round hidden corners of the playground. A girl gang who in our late teenage years – with our new-found feminism centred around anatomy in a way we now see as clearly problematic – dubbed ourselves 'The Vagaggles': a gaggle of vaginas. Poetic, I know.

Over the years we've pulled apart and been drawn back together. We've shared each other's secrets and shared one too many sexual partners. We went to different universities and made new friends and for some years spoke only every few months. We learned our politics from different places and still ended up believing in the same things. What are the chances that, fifteen years on, we're still bound by the same passions, humour and a fierce love for each other? Those chances seem pretty unlikely to me. Honestly, it sounds like soulmate stuff.

Yet the cultural narrative is that romantic – not platonic – love is the epitome of intimacy. I've certainly had a date or two who didn't understand why my friends' opinion of them carries just as much weight as my own. There's almost a sense that friendships are something you invest in until you find a romantic partner, who then becomes your priority. Girls' trips are things that happen before everyone settles down. Days and nights out with friends are inevitably replaced with dates. Platonic love comes second as soon as romantic love enters the picture.

But I think *Sabrina* and every other pop-culture reference that shows true love as two halves of a heart coming together has it wrong. A soulmate – as mine have taught me – is not necessarily someone who you intertwine every part of yourself with, or a person who completes you. Soulmates are people who are whole by themselves but who realize that running parallel to each other can create the most supportive, empowering and comforting kind of love there is.

And when we buy into the traditional narrative, not only do we miss out on the magic of platonic intimacy, we place our every need on to our romantic relationship to fulfil. We tell ourselves that if they're truly our soulmate, they should be able to provide us with everything we've ever wanted to feel, putting pressure on to something that's already unsteady (because romantic love always is).

Granted, there are a few feelings that my platonic soulmates aren't able to give me – first-date butterflies, the pure chemical rush of falling in love, the kind of sexual tension that buzzes through every cell in your body. But knowing how much connection exists with them means that I can explore dating to find those extra things, without needing the dates to necessarily give me everything else too. Romantic love doesn't feel like a replacement to the platonic kind to me, just a nice add-on to an already complete set. If I find a romantic soulmate in the future, this is how I hope it will be – like an expansion pack on *The Sims*, but instead of adding in pets, I'm adding in orgasms.

When I started dating again, one of the biggest challenges was simply presenting the new me. You have to know yourself to survive out there, and those dating-app bio prompts felt like a beaming torch into the parts I hadn't yet figured out. I'd been someone's girlfriend my entire adult life, I had no solid grasp on the woman I was now becoming. But every day that I spent with my friends I found a little bit more of her.

One night, I came home from a particularly hopeless internet date, and after five minutes cackling over every disastrous detail with my flatmate while making midnight snacks in the kitchen, I wondered why I'd even left the house. There was already such a rare kind of love living right there with me.

To me, that's what a soulmate feels like. Someone who I can find a home in but who would never let me settle there long enough to stop moving forward. Someone who sees me at my most broken, and still helps me hold on to a sense of who I am when I have my shit together. A soulmate feels like dancing round the house I grew up in singing 'A Whole New World', summers

A SOULMATE FEELS LIKE SOMEONE WHO I CAN'T IMAGINE MY LIFE WITHOUT. A SOULMATE FEELS LIKE BEING SEEN. AND IF I FEEL EVERY ONE OF THOSE THINGS WITH MY FRIENDS, WHY SHOULDN'T I CROWN THEM MY SOULMATES?

spent chasing boys on bumper cars, afternoons walking home from school and eating entire tubs of ice-cream together when I was scared of taking a bite on my own. A soulmate feels like someone who I can't imagine my life without. A soulmate feels like being seen.

And if I feel every one of those things with my friends, why shouldn't I crown them my soulmates?

Looking back to that early frost-covered morning when I was first starting to untangle the emotions of my relationship ending, I can see my brain was already starting to put my soul stone back together. Not mine and his, but theirs and mine. I'd always known that I had a beautifully rare kind of connection with my friends, but I didn't appreciate quite how beautiful until I took away the romantic love and they poured in to fill the gap. Sometimes I look back on the note I wrote that day, as the realization finally hit me, just to remind myself of how extraordinary this kind of love is. How world-shifting. How complete.

And if I could speak to the old, worried me on the verge of that break-up, I think I would use the words I wrote in that icy clearing . . .

You are surrounded by women who are so brilliant it sets your heart alight. Who are your intellectual equals, who share your humour, who read what you read and think what you're thinking before you've even said it. Who would drop their lives for you in a heartbeat and when they reach you they won't say the wrong things. Who know you – young you, sad you, vibrant you, grey you, hurt you, healed you – and love you. Do you really think that a man who allowed you to carry the relationship on your shoulders

*for eight years without offering to
share the weight is your soulmate?
You are surrounded by soulmates.*

ALISON MCGOVERN MP

The unique grief of losing a friend

Alison McGovern has been the Labour MP for Wirral South since 2010. She has served in the shadow government as Shadow City Minister, and in 2016 was elected co-chair of the all-party parliamentary group Friends of Syria. A tireless spokesperson on the human cost of the crisis, McGovern uses her platforms both in and outside the House of Commons to highlight the plight of Syrian civilians and refugees, and has been published in the **Financial Times,** *the* **Guardian** *and the* **Independent.** *Before being elected, she was a researcher in the House of Commons, and worked at Network Rail and the Art Fund.*

I can't go to Brighton without thinking of Jo. I can see her now, outside the Odeon cinema on the seafront, full of enthusiasm after being elected as MP for Batley and Spen. We already knew each other, but bumping into her there during the Labour Party conference in 2015 always sticks in my mind. Our political party had just been beaten at the polls, and I was feeling anxious and fearful. But new MPs bring new hope. Even when you have lost, everyone looks to the next generation. To change it, get it right this time, make it new again. To me, Jo Cox was one of those people. She was going to be that change. She made me feel hopeful.

I had known Jo since I was first elected, five years prior. Her husband, Brendan, worked for my then boss, Gordon Brown, and Jo worked alongside his wife, Sarah, campaigning for better maternal care in developing countries. Jo was the Chair of Labour Women's Network, too, and in charge of our feminist campaigns. We didn't know each other that well, but we believed in the same causes, and once she was elected to the Commons I got to know her better. While life had taken us to different places, like me she represented her hometown – we both were elected into front-line politics by the people we grew up with. And there were other connections, too – she had worked in international development for years, while I had been the shadow minister for international development.

The conversation on the Brighton seafront that day was classic Jo. I was very downhearted about the situation in Syria. So downhearted that I was telling her that nothing could be done to help the people under attack there. She smiled at me and listened, and then gave me a passionate argument about an alternative solution. I had already lived through the complexity and stress of trying to agree previous responses in Parliament, whereas Jo had not. They had been very difficult times. And I knew that such a proposal would be unlikely to win support from our colleagues. But Jo did not seem disheartened.

I so admired her persistence. Because, in truth, the similarities between us did not extend to our personalities. Jo was a natural optimist in life. If not a complete pessimist, I am at least a hard-faced realist. Jo was always out and about, climbing mountains, living on a boat, having adventures. I prefer books, a library, solitude. She was famous among our friends for hosting fantastic parties, and bringing people together, while I am infamous for hiding in the kitchen at said parties, hosting niche discussions about who will be the next governor of the Bank of England.

But once we were both in the Commons, our mutual passion for Syria brought us together. The situation was so serious, so disastrous, that we tried to join our very different skill sets in pursuit of

WHEN A PERSON DIES AT SUCH A PREMATURE POINT IN THEIR LIFE, WE CAN CELEBRATE ALL THAT WAS WONDERFUL ABOUT THEM, BUT WE CANNOT ESCAPE THE DEEP SENSE OF WRONG. THAT IS THE SIMPLE TRUTH. WHEN A FRIEND DIES TOO YOUNG, THERE IS NO OTHER WAY OF LOOKING AT IT.

ALISON MCGOVERN MP

bringing some care and attention to the vulnerable kids being bombed out of their homes. We became a tag team. Jo never gave in, and her bravery in the manner that she addressed the House was startling. She made it all so human, so moving, that even the stuffy House of Commons was punctured by a deep emotion when she spoke. I will always think of her on the green bench next to me.

Over the next year, the country faced so many political challenges and we talked often about what we could do, how we could change things for the better. In a place where friendship can be in short supply, Jo was right there. For us, the referendum on Britain's membership of the European Union in June 2016 felt like just the latest in a series of disasters.

And then Jo was murdered – four days before polling day, in her constituency, by a man with links to neo-Nazi parties.

*

Her death haunts me.

Losing a friend in such a public way was horrendous. I can only begin to imagine what it feels like for her children, her mum and dad, for Brendan and her sister, Kim. I am full of admiration for the way they have spoken about her and the causes she believed in. You can tell what incredibly good and dedicated people they all are, and how Jo's life must have been filled with love because of them.

But Jo's death haunts me because of the guilt. Perhaps this is always so when a friend loses a friend who is a similar age. She was killed at what should have been the beginning of a brilliant career, and a long life bringing up her kids. There is no fairness in that. When a person dies at such a premature point in their life, we can celebrate all that was wonderful about them, but we cannot escape the deep sense of wrong. That is the simple truth. When a friend dies too young, there is no other way of looking at it.

Worse, Jo's children are a similar age to my daughter. They are both wonderful – as Brendan said at the time, they have Jo's love hard-wired into them. But I have seen my daughter grow, and Jo has not. I wish so desperately that she could experience the many milestones I am witnessing. There are no words to describe the pain I feel on her behalf of not being able to see how wonderful they are.

In many ways I felt then, and I feel now, that she was a much better person than I am. Her death made me understand that life can be so fragile, that we are so much closer than we think to losing people who have so much to offer. And I felt so guilty that someone so good should be taken away. Jo's life was spent campaigning for the wellbeing of others. She had done brave things in pursuit of other people's interests. To lose her as a friend has been so painful, but this is compounded by a screaming sense of unfairness. It has been hard to bear.

In the immediate aftermath of Jo's death, I was in Westminster, and gathered work colleagues – fellow MPs and their staff – in the whips' office near to the House of Commons chamber so that no one would be alone. Rose, the Speaker's Chaplain, held people as they cried in shock and despair.

But a few of us had another job to do. Speaking out publicly is your job when you are a politician. And you speak out whether you want to or not. When you agree or disagree. When you have won or lost. My friend John told me that the media would want to hear from some of us. I was shaking with horror, but I tried to feel for whatever instincts were left. All I could think of was what would happen if the situation was reversed. Would I want Jo to tell people that I was her friend and that I was a good person, and that this was a

terrible, horrendous thing to have happened? Yes.
I would. And I think that Jo would have been
brave. So, attempting to channel her energy,
I faced the camera and tried to do my best to
explain to people who did not know Jo why they
should be inspired by her. I tried to explain what
she stood for – her passion for equality, for action
against injustice, for finding common ground, even
with those you disagree with.

Our friends matter to us not just because of the
company they provide or the support they give,
but because they can help us see where we are
falling short. In my grief, I realized my tendency to
hide my feelings, to struggle alone, was no good
to anyone. Jo would have responded to the
distress with practical help, and so should I. So I
tried to help others – Jo's friends, who were
equally crushed and broken. We had to get up
and keep campaigning for her. We had to follow
her lead.

IN MY GRIEF, I REALIZED MY TENDENCY TO HIDE MY FEELINGS, TO STRUGGLE ALONE, WAS NO GOOD TO ANYONE.

The next year was hard, and unexpected. Grief was constantly nearby. The trial of Jo's killer brought the realization home of how, and why, she was killed.

But unexpectedly, I felt my natural caution and fear begin to leave me. At times I felt hysterical. Literally the worst thing I could conceive of in politics had happened. I felt I no longer had anything to lose, like life had spun out of control. Sometimes I wanted to run away from it all, but mainly I didn't know what to do, so I decided to try to be more like Jo, as a person. To say yes to things, to try not to worry so much. If people asked me a question, I answered it straight.

I had become a Member of Parliament aged twenty-nine, and I had learned quickly that you should weigh your words. Politicians are notoriously calculating, always playing the game for advantage. I wouldn't say that I was Machiavellian, but I certainly knew when to keep my mouth shut. I was always conscious that I needed to prove myself, and was sensitive to the views of others.

After Jo was killed, my inner rebel burst out. I couldn't keep toeing the line. And though it sometimes felt like I had gone rogue, I just didn't care any more. I gave the honest answers I believed in, even on issues that many would consider controversial. I realized how fearful I had been before, but now I stopped caring if people criticized. What could anyone do to me? Jo's death was the worst. All else, I would just have to deal with.

As I lost inhibitions, I stopped feeling like such a closed-in version of myself. I was more open, more frank. What was the point any more of trying to hide my feelings? The only response was to take those feelings and build campaigns – in Jo's name, and in her honour – that she would have wanted us to fight for.

I have longed to talk to Jo about this shift in my attitude. Did she always know this was a better way to live?

On one of the campaigns I joined in the wake of Jo's death I met a woman called Eloise Todd. Eloise rang me one day to talk about it. Her Yorkshire accent – tempered by a few years working in Brussels – was just like Jo's. So was her ability to connect. I am wary of people by nature, but Eloise was disarming. I liked her and we talked for a long time on the phone. Eloise also told me about her friendship with Jo. She had been one of Jo's 'best women' (along with thirteen other alternative 'bridesmaids') and was part of Jo's big gang of pals from her years campaigning on global poverty. It was good to hear a voice just like my friend's talking about the things that she might have spoken to me about. It felt like comfort.

I do not have any faith. I do not believe in any sort of afterlife, in heaven, in a god, or in supernatural things. But I believe that the force of love that I felt from Jo somehow made me trust Eloise, though I barely knew her. The friend of my friend was here to help me, and I was here to help her. From that very first conversation, I felt at home in her company.

In the four years since Jo was murdered, politics has been incredibly eventful. I have felt the loss of her at every turn. I needed her feminist passion when men tried to shout me down about Europe, and I needed to tell her about the Syrian doctors I met who were trying to save lives in Idlib. Eloise's friendship means there is someone who knows. She knows how all this feels and understands so much without me having to explain. She has become a great friend.

*

In 2019, the Labour conference was back in Brighton. I thought about Jo as I walked along the front again. Her sister, Kim, had come to the conference to talk about the importance of listening to those you disagree with in politics, and I realized that the up and down of party politics means a lot less to me now. That instinct to embrace what is important and forget the rest is now embedded. While I regret much – especially losing Jo – this is the one aspect of change in my life over the past few years that I am truly grateful for. That is what I thought of as the waves hit the beach.

Grief has been an ongoing lesson. The intractable problems of today can disappear and the battles of tomorrow can be hard to imagine. Life is a journey and can be unexpected. You never know where the path will take you next, you just have to be wholehearted about it. Perhaps Jo knew this better than me, and that's why she was always up for adventure.

Losing a friend in the way that we lost Jo was horrendous, and all those who loved her miss her immeasurably. The comfort of each other, and the lessons of her life, are what we are left with. And they deserve to be cherished, as she was.

FELICITY THISTLETHWAITE

Why you should always tell your best friend if you're in love with them (by someone who did)

Felicity Thistlethwaite is Executive Editor Digital at Stylist. *Originally from Leicester, she read journalism at the University of Sheffield and began her career on a bi-annual fashion magazine where she was paid the princely sum of £50 a week. A former entertainment editor and showbiz reporter, she's interviewed David Attenborough twice, embarrassed herself in front of Usher once, and tussled on red carpets for quotes from Hollywood stars on countless occasions.*

We've all seen them – the feel-good films in which two friends realize they're falling in love, coyly confess their feelings to one another and, like the flick of a switch, live happily ever after (vom). Of course, nothing is ever as easy as Hollywood makes out, especially not risking rejection and eternal awkwardness from the most important person in your life. Take it from me, a woman who fell in love with her best friend and did absolutely nothing about it for almost a decade. But I'm here to tell you that speak up you should. Yes, even if it doesn't go your way. I'm also here to tell you that it might just be okay. Spoiler alert: Reader, I married him . . .

Aaron and I met at school when we were fourteen. He was already nearly six feet tall and super smart, but masked his natural intellect with an ill-fitting Adidas tracksuit and a propensity for shouting 'funny' remarks at top volume in class. I, on the other hand, was a more traditional waif-like nerd often carrying a white, hard-shell cello case on my back, which my classmates affectionately nicknamed 'The Coffin'.

Given the hierarchy of early-2000s high school – thank you, *Mean Girls* – our paths would never normally have crossed, so maybe it was fate that meant Aaron and I ended up together in most classes. I remember observing this hilarious, giant stranger from afar and thinking it wouldn't be a bad idea to get him on side. So I made a beeline to sit near him whenever the opportunity arose, and our unlikely friendship quickly blossomed.

Teenage friendships can be some of the most complicated relationships to navigate – it often feels like you're one chess move away from spending lunch break eating a sad sandwich alone in the toilet. But with Aaron it was so easy. Ours was a relationship built on taking the piss out of one another – something we were both good at. I'll never forget the day I slipped down a muddy bank at lunchtime in front of what felt like a Super Bowl-size crowd of rowdy teenagers, Aaron's laughter carrying across the school playing field. Cheers, mate.

Over time he became, in Maya Angelou's words, a rainbow on my cloud, whenever I needed cheering up. When anything bad happened, he was the first person I called. He was my stability, my grounded best friend who could coax me off any cliff edge.

Our friendship felt completely and utterly different to any friendship I'd had in the past. Was it because he was my first proper male friend? I often wondered. Or maybe it was because he was so laid back and easy-going. Either way, it was a friendship people on the outside rarely understood. And I can't really blame them. It was like watching a live-action remake of *Monsters, Inc.* when we walked into a party together: him Sulley; and me Mike. 'Do you fancy Aaron?' my female friends would often ask. I'd guffaw. 'Girls can be friends with boys, you know,' I'd say, rolling my eyes.

And I meant it. But two years into our friendship, I could sense something was changing. I wanted so desperately not to like him, but with every midnight text sent in the green glow of my Nokia 3310, I knew I was starting to fancy him.

Of course, I pushed my feelings to one side, telling myself it was just a crush. Thankfully, he appeared none the wiser. But by the time I was seventeen it was getting harder to smile and nod when Aaron introduced me to (yet another) new girlfriend. I was no Mother Teresa, but good lord, that man had a harem of women – I blame it on him being one of the first in our friendship group to own a car. Nothing says sophistication like a 1995 Vauxhall Corsa with alloy wheels.

As we all went from young-teenagers-who-were-mates to hardened-teens-who-wanted-to-snog-people, our friendship was constantly under the microscope. Perhaps the others could see something we couldn't. More likely it was just pervasive gender norms at play. Either way, the pressure of being best friends who had to constantly deny feelings for one another was starting to show on both of us. Aaron and I had reached a fork in the road.

I often look back and wonder why, when we'd practically been crowned Leicester's very own Ross and Rachel anyway, I didn't speak up. But that's the thing about telling a friend you're in love with them: all you can see before you is the barriers. Even without teenage angst at play, it leaves you horribly vulnerable. It perhaps wasn't the smartest place to look for relationship advice, but I often had the words of Billy Crystal's character in *When Harry Met Sally* ringing in my ears at this time. 'No man can be friends with a woman that he finds attractive. He always wants to have sex with her,' he tells Sally. Well, Aaron seemed to be doing a pretty good job of being friends with me. Did I really need him to turn me down out loud?

All I knew was that, at seventeen, I valued our friendship so much that I wasn't willing to risk it for anything, even as I realized I didn't just find him attractive, I was falling in love . . .

In the end, my hand was forced just after I finished my A levels. We went to the local Odeon to watch *Casino Royale*, Aaron picking me up in his car. But something felt different. It didn't feel like two mates going to see a film, it felt awkward . . . like a date. I realized that he wasn't taking the piss out of me. Even weirder, we were both trying to say nice things to each other. If his intention was to put a halt to the banter and dial up the compliments to try and woo me, it had failed. But the idea that he was trying to woo me excited me all the same . . .

I'll never forget the moment he pulled up outside my parents' house to drop me off after two and a half of the most uncomfortable hours of my life. If those dodgy Hollywood movies about friends falling in love had made me believe one thing, it's that there's always *a moment*. And this, I realized, as I leaned across to say goodbye, was mine. I needed to make a move . . . but I completely bottled it. Aaron drove off, I sloped inside and our friendship crumbled in the moonlight.

That night had been so weird that even without any confession of love there was no coming back from it as best friends. It was all too much. We quietly drifted apart and, for the next few years, we barely spoke.

During that time I decided Harry was wrong – a man, or woman, for that matter, could be friends with a person they found attractive. Hurrah! The real issue is that it's impossible to be friends with a person you've fallen in *love* with. You either step back because it's too painful, or you just bloody tell them. Either way, it's the end of your friendship as you know it.

In our early twenties, we started to gradually rekindle our friendship with the odd friendly 'like' on Facebook. I'd resigned myself to the fact that I'd always hold a candle for Aaron but he'd never be more than a friend, so when we started spending more time together I was happy, but had no expectations. We'd both grown up: he had a full-time job and I was at university. Everything was the same, but also completely different.

This time, I made sure Aaron had to listen to me talking about guys I was dating. I wanted him to know I was thriving without him. But the reality was that I'd get drunk and this facade would slip.

I'd whisper to my university friends that I was in love with Aaron, and they'd knowingly nod and line up another shot at the bar. Whenever I asked their advice about what to do, they were divided. And, as ever, the only place I ever pitched a tent was the 'chronic fear of rejection' camp. Even if you do get a green light, I'd wail, what if you kiss – or worse, have sex – and it all just feels too weird? No, I wasn't about to risk my already weakened friendship with Aaron a second time.

A few more years went by like this. He went travelling, I moved to London for work and was loving the single life. One evening, a message from him dropped into my inbox. 'It's only been like 5 days since we had a gd chat n i miss u already! wtf is wrong with me???' he wrote. It wasn't exactly Shakespearian prose, but it gave me those horribly familiar butterflies I'd had back when we would text on our old Nokia phones.

Then, something changed. He had decided his time travelling was up, he was flying home and had a job interview in London. Could he come and stay with me for a night?

I sent a mass text to my friends, and then I prepared to do what I should've done back in

2006 in that clapped-out Corsa. We weren't teenagers any more, and we didn't have the same all-consuming friendship. I had the job I'd always wanted, a brilliant set of friends – there was just one thing missing: him. Really, there was almost nothing to lose.

So, on that random Tuesday night, Aaron and I talked and joked for a solid six hours, until 1 a.m. It really was just like old times. But this time I was certain – there was definitely a spark.

After getting changed into our PJs, I thought fuck it, and kissed him in the pitch black. If he'd pushed me away, I'd have been mortified, but I'd spent too many years being held hostage by my own insecurities.

Once we got that first kiss out of the way it was all totally natural. I felt a scramble of emotions when Aaron admitted that he also fell in love with me as a teenager. 'Think how much anguish we could have saved each other!' I screeched. But how could I blame him for being as scared as I was? In truth, it was a comfort to know he'd cherished our friendship as much as me.

Seven years after our first kiss, on April Fool's Day 2018, Aaron asked me to marry him, and in 2019 we said our vows in front of a small group of our closest friends and family in Norfolk. Do I regret not saying something sooner? Well, yes. It was such a relief to have it all out in the open, and I couldn't have been happier. But considering our ages, we both agree it was no bad thing – who's to say a relationship begun at sixteen would have lasted the course?

Still, if I could talk to 2006 Fliss as she applied her final layer of Juicy Tube lip gloss before the cinema, I'd tell her this: of course there's a risk that revealing your feelings could ruin the good thing you've got going, but *not* acknowledging those feelings will ultimately end your friendship, anyway. Hiding your true feelings means you're not

THERE'S A RISK THAT REVEALING YOUR FEELINGS COULD RUIN THE GOOD THING YOU'VE GOT GOING, BUT *NOT* ACKNOWLEDGING THOSE FEELINGS WILL ULTIMATELY END YOUR FRIENDSHIP, ANYWAY. HIDING YOUR TRUE FEELINGS MEANS YOU'RE NOT ONLY LYING TO YOURSELF – YOU'RE LYING TO YOUR BEST FRIEND TOO.

only lying to yourself – you're lying to your best friend too. And that's a recipe for disaster. No stable friendship is built on a bed of lies, and Aaron and I nailed a huge wedge between us by hiding our emotions.

No, not every Ross is going to find their Rachel, and not every Ron will snog their Hermione. But the happiest of times *can* come from making the hardest decisions. Trust your friend to be gentle if they don't feel the same way and understand that, in reality, friendships change all the time. It's futile ignoring your feelings to maintain something that will likely change anyway, regardless of what you do.

And yes, if the person you're in love with doesn't love you back, your friendship probably won't go back to what it once was. But would you want it to? There's no way I'd have been able to stand by and watch Aaron carve out a life for himself with another person. Jealousy would've got the better of me, as it would almost any human being.

It's a gamble, sure. But the biggest risk of all, I realized, is risking nothing. Because that way, you end up risking everything.

DAME JENNI MURRAY

Friends for life: how it feels to find the one

One of Britain's most respected, award-winning broadcasters – and recognizable voices – Dame Jenni Murray has presented BBC Radio 4's Woman's Hour *since 1987. Known for her feminist values and fearlessness in tackling controversial topics, she's also fronted* Newsnight *and the* Today *programme, written eight books and makes frequent contributions to* The Times, *the* Daily Mail *and the* Guardian. *She holds honorary degrees from a number of universities, including St Andrews, London, Salford and, most recently, Chester, and was awarded an OBE for services to broadcasting in 1999. In 2011 she was appointed Dame Commander of the Order of the British Empire (DBE).*

'Oh, look at those two,' we'd often say, as a pair of old women came into our favourite restaurant, where we met regularly for a night out and a good gossip. 'It's so sweet.' We were not being patronizing, but, as two relatively young women in our thirties, we were delighting in such demonstrations of long and clearly intimate friendships.

The older women were sharing something that had obviously been a joy and a comfort to them for a lifetime: a best friend with whom they could talk about absolutely anything – husbands, lovers, children, jobs, success, failure, happiness and grief – without fear of criticism or censure. Looking on back then, a friendship that had survived so much felt like an achievement and something to aspire to. Now, almost forty years later, I know that it is indeed both those things. And that it's built in the highs and lows of everyday life, the product of mutual support rather than always being each other's mirror image.

Sally and I met through work. She was the deputy editor of *Woman's Hour* in 1987 when I first joined the programme as presenter. The connection between us was instantaneous. We each had children of similar ages – mine were two boys, Ed and Charlie; hers were a boy and a girl, Ricky and Scarlett. We were equally committed to feminist politics and had managed to bag ourselves a couple of kind, decent men who had no difficulty with us taking on the role of breadwinner while they, as my David would joke, literally made the bread.

Sally's brilliance and sense of humour made her the best editor any presenter could hope for. We only once came close to falling out. In 1991 William Kennedy Smith, a nephew of President Kennedy, was tried for rape and the trial was broadcast in America. The alleged victim had been interrogated brutally in court and we planned a discussion about whether her humiliation should have been shown so openly.

Sally thought we shouldn't play an extract and repeat the insult to the young woman. I listened to the material and thought it important that our audience should hear how awful her treatment had been. We argued and argued and, finally, I managed to persuade Sally to listen to the toe-curlingly painful questioning she had endured. I won!

Kennedy was acquitted, but I still believe we were right to demonstrate how badly a woman making an accusation of rape can be rubbished by a clever and expensive defence attorney. Happily, Sally agrees.

For ten years we were the closest of work colleagues as our friendship deepened day by day. We worked hard and we played hard. It was Sally's genius as a mover and shaker that protected

Woman's Hour when, in 1991, the then channel controller decided to move us from the 2 o'clock slot it had inhabited since 1946 and floated the idea of making it a general magazine programme, maybe 'The Jenni Murray Show'. We were united in our belief that it was a bad idea. Sally hired, free of charge, a marketing specialist, who came with us to a meeting and laid out a most persuasive argument, formulated, as I recall, by her. It's not a good idea, the controller was told, to change the name of a loved and trusted product. Jammie Dodgers might alter their packaging. Marks & Spencer might move to a different store down the street. The brand name remains. We lost the 'time' argument, but the name and content stayed the same.

My admiration for my friend knew no bounds. As a manager, she was beyond comparison, and as an inspiring editor, always teeming with ideas, she shone. Her admiration for me was equally apparent. It was a great foundation for a friendship – respect for our very different but complementary talents. No competition and no jealousy.

There is one subject on which we have never agreed, though, which came to the fore on a trip to Bath. We had decided to make a programme there in celebration of the 180th anniversary of the publication of Jane Austen's first novel, *Sense and Sensibility*. She's a favourite author of both of us.

On the train I was busy writing an article and Sally was making preparations for the following day's programme. As we arrived in Bath we got off the train in something of a kerfuffle and, as it pulled out of the station, I realized I'd left my small suitcase behind containing everything necessary for an overnight stay, plus smart clothes to wear in front of the audience the next morning. Panic! The station manager called through to the next station, Bristol. They searched the carriage we'd occupied. Nothing. The case had gone.

'Not to worry,' said Sally. 'Every cloud and all that. We can have some fun shopping. We'll get it sorted.' She loves to shop. She adores glamorous clothes. Her father ran a company which manufactured fashion, so she grew up with it. I detest it all, happy with a few simple tops in pretty drab colours, a series of plain black trousers or leggings and rather dull, preferably flat shoes.

She dragged me mercilessly around the shops, did everything she could to cheer me up and made me (yes, *made* me) buy a V-necked sweater in a dark colour with gold thread running through it and a gold tiger embroidered on the chest. She loved it. I wore it for the programme and never again. She simply cannot understand my indifference to the dictates of fashion or my hatred of shopping. And I'm just as bewildered by her passion for it.

In the early nineties my family and I moved our main home to the Peak District. I kept a small basement flat in London, fondly known as Wuthering Depths, for the purpose of having somewhere to sleep during the working week and proximity to our favourite restaurant, the Camden Brasserie. Sally and I would continue our frequent evenings out together, but weekends with husbands and children were to transfer to the North.

Sally's daughter, Scarlett, still recalls their first visit to our farm. She reminded me the other day of Sally, North London born and bred, preparing for the countryside with a pair of very fancy and entirely impractical gold trainers. Sally looked out of our kitchen window at the stunning landscape and shrieked, 'But where are the shops?' I almost had to deliver CPR after her breathless response to my reply: 'Oh, the nearest is more than three miles away, but it's only a little village store!'

She got over it and learned to enjoy our family reunions, the friendships the children developed, the games (I never did master the bridge at which she and the husbands were adept), the open fires and the hours spent gossiping around my kitchen table with a glass or more of wine.

Truth be told, there were times when our tendency to play hard got a little out of control. The programme's move to the morning had enabled us to go out to lunch together. I could never quite match her phenomenal ability to enjoy her wine and then go back and be perfectly effective in the office. It must have been around that time that we began to discuss 'the five most dangerous words in the English language': *shall we open another bottle?*

I'm afraid, to the alarm of our husbands and children, we often did. I was one of the first people to see the very first episode of *Absolutely Fabulous*, to be broadcast in 1992. I had a preview copy in preparation for an interview with the sitcom's creator, Jennifer Saunders, and began watching it with my older boy, Ed, who was nine at the time.

Edina Monsoon, played by Saunders, fell out of a taxi, staggered drunkenly into her house and fell into bed surrounded by wine glasses and overflowing ashtrays. Ed literally fell off the sofa, howling with laughter. 'Mum!' he said. 'Did you and Sally write this?'

Of course, we were not quite so badly behaved, but we loved the show, joked a lot about 'being Patsy and Edina' and wished we could afford to be as free with the Bolly as they were. Only Sally hankered after the fondness for Harvey Nicks the fictional characters shared.

So there was lots of fun, but there were tough periods too. It really is true that the test of a great and enduring friendship accompanies the worst rather than the best of times.

One of ours came in 1997. Sally had long ago been promoted to the position of editor of *Woman's Hour*, and the audience was rising. But new management came on board, changed the description of the editor's job, made Sally apply, and she didn't get it.

Quite rightly, she packed away her stuff and, furious and heartbroken, left the building. That night she came to me in Wuthering Depths. We went to the Brasserie for dinner, returned to the flat, wept and screamed out our anger, got horribly drunk and played Carole King's album *Tapestry* over and over again. Sally being Sally, she bounced back pretty quickly and soon had a well-paid job in academia. My working life was never the same again.

The friendship more than survived, though. I had breast cancer first. In 2006 she was the first to call as I came out of the anaesthetic. She claims I told her a mastectomy was marvellous and everyone should have one. I must have been high as a kite on morphine, and remember nothing.

She was diagnosed in 2010, and recalls her phone ringing as she opened the doors to the hospital on her way to treatment. It was me reassuring her that everything would be fine.

Those moments underscored an unspoken rule of any great friendship: *always be available for her*. In all honesty, while I'm well aware that staying in touch is so vital to nurturing such a bond, to my shame, it's the thing at which I am, frankly, hopeless. Sally is brilliant at it. Even now, at least once a fortnight I get a call, an email or a text asking me when I'll be free for dinner. But whenever something *major* has happened in our lives, we've always both been there in a flash to support each other. That's the deep comfort of having one special friend – it's with her you can share secrets and intimacies you would reveal to no one else and know she can be trusted completely. Rugby players have a saying which is about trust and confidence: 'What goes on tour stays on tour.' A best female friend knows that instinctively.

RUGBY PLAYERS HAVE A SAYING WHICH IS ABOUT TRUST AND CONFIDENCE: 'WHAT GOES ON TOUR STAYS ON TOUR.' A BEST FEMALE FRIEND KNOWS THAT INSTINCTIVELY.

I can recall countless examples of us leaning on each other when we needed it most; lifts from Sally when I could barely walk as a result of dodgy hips, food brought round when I broke my humerus in a fall on December ice, compassion and comfort when our long-term relationships threatened to hit the buffers . . . But, most memorably, a trip to the West End to see the Carole King musical, *Beautiful*.

It was the night before I was due to go into hospital for metabolic surgery – a gastric sleeve which would help my weight loss. I had become dangerously obese. Sally had booked the tickets and we sat together in the stalls, listening to those favourite songs that had comforted us on that terrible night in 1997. As the song we loved the best – 'You've Got a Friend' – was performed, we glanced at each other, held hands and sobbed. It could have been written for us, echoing our unspoken promises over many years that all we had to do was call and that wherever we were, we'd come running. There was no need to say anything. The lyrics said it all.

Our old favourite restaurant, the Camden Brasserie, has long gone now, but we've built up half a dozen places to continue our catch-ups where the food is good and the atmosphere congenial. Often I'll catch sight of a pair of thirty-something friends and smile. What lessons could I share with them from nearly forty years of a truly best friendship? Certainly that female friends are vital, as they get you as no man can. And while there'll be lots of pleasurable acquaintances in life, one special best friend has an incalculable value. Sustaining it means you must never let a partner get in the way, though. The lover may not last, as sex and romance can complicate matters. A best friend will be for ever.

But the best thing about those meals together – as it always has been – is spending time with the person who shares my history, my values and

WHILE THERE'LL BE LOTS OF PLEASURABLE ACQUAINTANCES IN LIFE, ONE SPECIAL BEST FRIEND HAS AN INCALCULABLE VALUE. SUSTAINING IT MEANS YOU MUST NEVER LET A PARTNER GET IN THE WAY, THOUGH. THE LOVER MAY NOT LAST, AS SEX AND ROMANCE CAN COMPLICATE MATTERS. A BEST FRIEND WILL BE FOR EVER.

politics and who will always be there for me, no matter what. And of course wondering if the younger women in the restaurant are looking at us and thinking, 'Oh, look at those two old friends!' I just hope they don't call us 'sweet'.

CANDICE BRATHWAITE

The best friend I've never met

Candice Brathwaite is the author of **Sunday Times** *bestseller* **I Am Not Your Baby Mother (2020),** *a part memoir, part manifesto about black British motherhood. On a mission to show that young black families aren't just surviving, but thriving, she campaigns for a more accurate and inclusive depiction of motherhood in the media, and has kickstarted national conversations about maternal mortality rates for black women in Britain. A frequent spokesperson on* **BBC News,** *Radio 4, and at* **Stylist** *Live and the Hay Festival, she is also founder of online initiative Make Motherhood Diverse. Candice lives in Milton Keynes with her partner, Bodé, and two young children.*

Perhaps it was because I was out cycling that I didn't hear the doorbell ring. I've got one of those RING doorbells, you see. I get sent a lot of packages because of my job and online shopping habit, so it helps to be able to tell a delivery guy where to leave them if I'm not in. But as I entered the house and saw the box sitting on the love seat I screwed up my face in surprise. 'A slow cooker?' I thought to myself. 'Where on earth did that come from?'

I asked Papa B (the nickname I have for my other half), who just shrugged in his 'hey, it's you who does online shopping at 3 a.m.' type way, and left me to it. But once I'd opened the box it all became clear. I knew where it had come from. It was sent by my dear friend Emma. True to form, she'd remembered that the month of March is jam-packed with birthdays in our house. It was only the beginning of February – as ever, she was ahead of the curve. Rather than sending a slow cooker, she had cunningly used an old box to house a grotto's worth of presents for the entire family.

'Oh, Emma.' I smiled, running my hand along the notebook she had picked for me, inscribed with a quote that was exceptionally timely. Just like her. In the three or so years I had known her, she'd displayed an uncanny knack for messaging me just as I felt I had no gas left in the tank, or sending across a pick-me-up when life seemed to be spinning out of control. Aside from the notebook, there were toys and books for the kids and a gift voucher for Papa B to re-up on his favourite tipple. That's what I love about Emma: she's always thinking about – well, everyone. She has a huge heart and is not just a dear friend to me but considered a close friend by the whole family. I hadn't even given the children all the presents 'Auntie' Emma had sent for Christmas for fear that they would become spoilt and expectant. But whenever I mentioned that to her she'd simply say, 'That's what I'm here to do' – adding that it makes her happy that they're happy.

Not that she sees the kids actually play with their birthday presents, you understand. Or ever comes to any of our birthday parties. She wasn't there two summers ago either, when I threw quite the lavish garden party to celebrate my thirtieth. Of course I wanted to invite her, but I then thought better of it. Let's be honest, meeting someone so special for the first time in such a setting would make anyone's stomach flip.

Oh, hadn't I mentioned? I've never actually *met* Emma. And if I'm being honest, there is a strong chance I never will.

You see, Emma and I met online. More specifically, via Instagram. I know saying that just made a few eyebrows raise to the heavens, and that some will now doubt the true depth of our friendship. But why? While ours is a written rather than verbal relationship, we interact every day, sharing everything from family news to our private fears. Why are we so used to swiping right when looking for a potential significant other, yet still squeamish about using similar platforms to make friends – in the true sense of the word? Heightened sexual exchanges with someone you meet online are deemed totally acceptable, while making a platonic friend is seen as dodgy, maybe even delusional. And yet my friendship with Emma is one of the most genuine relationships in my life.

Despite meeting via our phones, I instantly felt a connection – and I think she would say the same. She is smart – whip-smart, in fact. She is exceptionally well read and, from the very beginning, showed a genuine kindness that seemed to penetrate through the screen. I can't actually remember the distinct moment when we went from just commenting and liking each other's pictures to considering each other friends, but I know I became even more enamoured with her once she did a virtual takeover for another Instagram platform I run, called Make Motherhood Diverse.

The platform seeks to offer a more diverse and inclusive representation of motherhood, and we often encourage women to lend their voices to that space. All the women who share on that platform are courageous, but Emma's takeover was especially so because she physically isn't able to have children. She has Ehlers-Danlos Syndrome, a group of disorders that affect the connective tissues, causing a range of symptoms from mildly loose joints to life-threatening complications. One of those complications for Emma is that should she get pregnant, her body would abort her child.

Watching her share this painful truth so publicly made my heart swell and then break into millions of pieces. When I hear quotes or script-like platitudes about remaining gracious and hopeful even in the face of adversity, Emma always comes to mind. Even though she is unable to have her own children, she still interacts with and supports women who are perhaps living a life that she once dreamed about. And, for me, she has become a guiding star, the kind of friend you can't imagine your life without.

Even without the restrictions of her illness, I am acutely aware that if it wasn't for the online space, and more specifically social media, Emma and I might have never connected with each other. Social media has a bad rap for encouraging us to live in an echo chamber, but it can also help break down barriers and introduce us to people we would never cross paths with IRL.

And, for me, that would have been a true shame. Not just because Emma is one of life's good ones but because, perhaps without even knowing it, she challenges me to not only see the good in people but to continue to try and give the best of myself even when it seems that the circumstances are not in my favour. I suspect she wasn't feeling her best when she sent that box of presents – a mutual friend of ours had just died, leaving behind three very young children. In those traumatic few weeks, we'd both been reminded how fragile this thing called life really is. Yet Emma still made the effort to reach out, to tighten our bond, and with her gifts reminded me that it's important to show love in any way that you can.

This isn't to say that online friendships are always a pixellated bed of roses. I perhaps more than most have learned that the hard way. Yes, you could be in communication with someone you really don't know at all, and with cat fishing and false identities being an increasing menace, it's important to proceed with caution. I know many people who are suspicious of bonding online: 'How can you be sure that she is who she says she is?' they ask. And true – aside from our virtual trail of emails and texts, and of course the presents and cards, there's lots that I don't know about Emma. I've only heard her voice via Insta Stories, I've never been to her house or felt heat radiate from her actual body. But still, I've always been inclined to trust her.

Why? Perhaps it's because I've had friendships with people I physically embraced who were pretty vicious once my back was turned. I've had decade-long friendships which have ended at a moment's notice because it turned out I didn't know that person at all. I've learned that IRL interactions come with no guarantee either.

So I refuse to let a few bad apples spoil the harvest. After all, it's not like making friends gets any easier as we get older. I remember when it used to be as simple as a swift exchange of a friendship bracelet or helping someone reset their Tamagotchi. But after leaving the playground and becoming an adult, making friends seems a very complicated thing indeed.

Perhaps it was easier when we were inclined to remain in one job and one city for years on end. Friendships could be established over time, and reaffirmed almost effortlessly by close and constant contact. But in our increasingly global world, and with most of the people I know either freelancing like me or hot-desking, the only recurring person in our lives is the cute guy making our coffee or the woman delivering our Amazon Prime orders.

Not that most of us have time to stand around chatting and checking out potential new mates anyway. Twenty-first-century life is b-u-s-y. Add in a career, family commitments, a time-sapping commute, and suddenly a friendship that exists only on your phone begins to sound eminently sensible. Even if you've signed up to, say, a group exercise class with the intention of making new friends, between giving it your all in downward-facing dog and trying to get home in time to make a healthy meal (you don't want to undo all your hard work, after all), there's not much time to be searching for a new bestie. Quite frankly, at this stage in my life, I'm grateful for any short cuts or ways to meet new people.

So how exciting to think that a wealth of new friends could quite literally be at our fingertips! Even with my track record of being a little too trusting and sometimes getting my heart broken, I'm ever the optimist about the joy of a new connection. As with falling in love, there is so much joy in the early days. The endless messages! The discovery that she, too, also knows every line in *Clueless*! God, just thinking about all those things puts a smile on my face. And so, although to many outsiders my friendship with Emma may seem juvenile or borderline pretend, I value it just as much, if not more so, than the friendships that society views as more conventional.

And maybe it's just me, but conventional friendships are bound by so many – well, conventions. While they can provide a healthy framework, all those expectations can sometimes end up feeling like a straitjacket. I love the freedom that an online friendship brings. At the start at least, the only place you meet is online, as and when you choose to be there. It's totally on your terms. If Emma hasn't seen me online or had a text from me for a while, she will reach out, as she knows it isn't like me to go off-grid for too long. And I do the same for her. But there are no false expectations of a weekly Saturday meet-up, or pressure to go for a coffee every time you bump into each other at the school gates. Truth be told, now I know Emma so well, I hope we can one day meet up, but when I've gently floated the idea she has politely sidestepped it, so I've respectfully left it there. And, in fact, I'd say that it's because it isn't rooted in the ordinary that my relationship with

I LOVE THE FREEDOM THAT AN ONLINE FRIENDSHIP BRINGS. AT THE START AT LEAST, THE ONLY PLACE YOU MEET IS ONLINE, AS AND WHEN YOU CHOOSE TO BE THERE. IT'S TOTALLY ON YOUR TERMS.

Emma has room to be extraordinary. There is, I think, a special type of authenticity that only a certain level of anonymity can bring. I perhaps wouldn't feel comfortable discussing my financial stresses with a work friend for fear of where that information will land, but I never think twice about having a good old moan to Emma.

Maybe, I believe not just in Emma but our friendship so much because the ones that come with selfies in a nightclub or meeting for lunch every other day to gossip have lost some of their shine. Or, should I say, gained an agenda. For all its many positives, there's no doubt that social media can skew our idea of what 'friendship' really means. Many of us have been duped into thinking that chasing more followers can replace what we are actually lacking, which is true connection. And yet, ironically, I would go so far as to say that there is perhaps more depth and honesty to be found in an online friendship like ours – because it isn't for

THERE IS PERHAPS MORE DEPTH AND HONESTY TO BE FOUND IN AN ONLINE FRIENDSHIP LIKE OURS – BECAUSE IT ISN'T FOR SHOW. IT HAPPENS BEHIND CLOSED DOORS, BEHIND A SCREEN, WHERE WE CAN BOTH BE OURSELVES: NO EXPECTATIONS, NO PRESSURE, NO AGENDA. IT'S NOT BEING HELD TO ANYONE'S STANDARDS. IT'S OURS ALONE.

show. It happens behind closed doors, behind a screen, where we can both be ourselves: no expectations, no pressure, no agenda. It's not being held to anyone's standards. It's ours alone.

Emma is loyal. She's kind. We make each other laugh and cheer each other on. She shows up in the good and bad moments of not just her own life but mine too. I've got her and she's got me. And while I might not know the smell of her perfume or the squidginess of her sofa, there's one thing I know for sure. We don't have to share the same air space to be true friends.

FLO PERRY

Why I'll always need queer friends

Flo Perry is a much-loved illustrator and author, with a penchant for drawing boobs and cats. A former BuzzFeed editor and self-appointed sexpert, she is the author of How to Have Feminist Sex: A Fairly Graphic Guide *(2019), and illustrator of* Remember This When You're Sad *(2018) and* The Girls' Guide to Growing Up Great *(2018). Through her humorous yet searingly relatable comic-style illustrations, which often go viral, and speaking engagements at global events like WOW festival, she champions more honest conversations around sex, body confidence and feminism. A proud bisexual, she lives in North London, where she grew up, with her girlfriend, two flatmates and a cat.*

My best friend in the world is also gay. We made friends in Year 9, after eyeing each other suspiciously from either side of the cafeteria for two years. I came out two years later, she came out six years after that. I always think of it as tremendous luck that we both turned out to be massive dykes. Not only are we platonic soulmates who grew up together and know each other's lives inside out, but she has now also finally watched the whole of The L Word. We grew up in the same place, had the same friends, and even did the same A levels. But we have two unique experiences of what it's like to be queer. In fact, there isn't much that bonds the whole queer community together - friendship is certainly not guaranteed! Often it can feel as though we are constantly disagreeing. About what rights we should be fighting for next, about what Pride should look like, about who we should include in our community. So why do I want to pay tribute to my gay friends here? Because, really, there is only one thing that every queer person has experienced. Something that others struggle to see, let alone understand. Without my queer friends, everyday moments like this would be that little bit harder...

But everyone is queer! I don't wanna be mistaken for someone looking to have a threesome with their boyfriend.

Say you're bisexual then?

But I haven't dated a man in years, and even though I slept with Chris at the office party last year, I can't actually imagine being with a man. I'm just too gay. What do you think about bisexual lesbian?

I think it totally undermines what it actually means to be a lesbian. Why do you need to prove how minutely different you are from everyone else with an undercut, anyway? Can't you just call yourself gay?

KATHERINE ORMEROD

The joy of having few friends

Frank, honest and always impeccably dressed, journalist turned influencer Katherine Ormerod is a trailblazing voice on style, social media culture and contemporary womanhood. Her TEDx Talk (2019) and book, **Why Social Media is Ruining Your Life** *(2018), were prompted by her own experiences of navigating online pressures, but she is equally known for her intelligent fashion insights, having spent fifteen years on* **Sunday Times Style**, **Grazia** *and* **Glamour**. *Committed to empowering women through honest communication, Katherine edits workworkwork. co, an anti-perfectionism platform, runs her own brand consultancy and is fearless in starting important conversations on her popular Instagram account, tackling everything from maternity discrimination to sustainable fashion.*

As I'm a thirty-six-year-old woman who has been popular professionally for over fifteen years, it wouldn't be outlandish to assume I must have a well-established social life. Working as a fashion journalist, I meet different faces old and new for breakfast, lunch or dinner every single week of the year. Through my career in social media, I speak to countless people online, with sixty thousand of them choosing to follow me on a daily basis. I have had seven staff jobs in the same city, each with a huge pool of potential friends, and outside of work I've lived within the same mile radius since 2011. Plus, I ticked all the early motherhood boxes after having my son two years ago, paying for budding new buddies at NCT, so no excuses there either. In truth, there's been an embarrassment of opportunities to build a solid squad. So surely I'm kicking back into middle age on a cosy-kitchen-supper circuit with my tight network of forever friends. Right?

Well, turns out: wrong. I'm never Billy no-mates, but I can count my close friends on the fingers of one hand. That motley line-up would certainly never constitute a squad either – most of them haven't even met each other. While there is a certain red thread connecting them (an unusually large capacity for Pinot Noir) and we could all have a lovely lunch together, there are none of those shared experiences, memories or regular social events to bind us together. It's more a collection of strangers who only really have me in common.

A further eyebrow raiser, or so I've noticed, is the fact that I don't really have anyone in my life who knew me before I turned thirty. I have a lovely lone schoolfriend I check in with a couple of times a year and two amazing uni friends I WhatsApp with, but there's a gap where that rabble of old school and uni friends – ex-housemates, lab partners and year-abroad cohorts – 'should' be. I don't go on coupled-up weekends away, get asked to many baby showers, birthday soirées or any of those Hallmark friendship moments which I'd expected to fill this phase of my life. Truth be told, on most Friday nights I'm home, drinking the other half of the bottle I opened on Tuesday, with Netflix thrumming mindlessly in the background. I might have Facetimed my friend Beth in New York, or spent most of the day with my pal Cami. But by the evening, my boyfriend may or may not be playing *Red Dead Redemption II* and I could quite possibly be knitting.

Does that sound sad? At times I've thought so too. After all, according to *Girls*, *Sex and the City* and Taylor Swift, we're all meant to be 'squadded up' – a gang of gfs, a network of ride or dies. Just recently I read in a self-help book that you shouldn't trust people with no old friends, and while it sounds eminently sensible to be wary of those who lack the capacity to maintain long friendships, it doesn't do much for the ol' self-esteem.

And yet, there has been a litany of circumstances that helps explain my own bijou list of friends. After A levels in London, a move to university in Edinburgh at the same time as my mum sold our family home and upped sticks to Cape Town put the kibosh on my teenage friendships. A few years later, a hugely demanding new career and all-encompassing relationship with my soon-to-be husband (I was engaged at twenty-four) similarly worked to cut most ties post-graduation. I'd put eight years of hard graft into my CV before I met any of my current solid speed dials, which definitely doesn't tally with conventional narratives of when your friends are 'supposed' to be made. And yet I'd bet my set-up is far more common than Hollywood and apparently every account on Instagram would have us believe. Those normative ideas of friendship ignore some fundamental truths about modern life: many of us go through major life changes which shift our relationships. Even if you dip your toe in, that squad status quo can't always be maintained.

The next seismic wave of my own life came just shy of my thirtieth, when my husband left me. Prior to that, I'd been somewhat ensconced in an extended group of married friends. My life, at least on the surface, was following a more well-trodden friend trajectory (one summer I attended nine weddings, just in case we're counting). But those friends were mainly my ex's, and after the split I realized how incredibly caught up I'd been in our relationship and his life, as one by one they quickly fell away, in a manner that anyone going through a painful break-up might be familiar with.

Post split, I was lonely as hell, but rebuilding my social life basically from scratch, it became clear that I had changed significantly. Now in my thirties, post divorce, I finally knew myself and had an idea of the kind of friends I wanted around me – after all, you are the company you keep.

Slowly, I began to appreciate that it was actually something of a gift to get to choose the people who I connected with as a developed adult. I was aware of the character traits I most admire in a friend, and could curate accordingly.

As a result, my chums are all plain-speaking, self-confident, layered and sharp. They all have a great sense of humour and have chosen the road less travelled. Like me, they've all been expats (well, Bethie lives thousands of miles away from her hometown on the opposite coast, so close enough) and have the sense of independence that comes with building a life away from their families, high schools and the expectations of others. They are, in short, the opposite of friends of convenience – as my Friday nights attest. Take my friend Cami, for instance. Even though we see each other five days out of seven, she'll generally disappear to make mischief once the sun sets. Our life stages aren't in synch (she's five years younger than me, and I one thousand per cent can't keep up), which is totally normal when you don't hang out with people from school. And yet our connection is real.

It's a similar story with Kelly – the friend with whom I probably have most in common. We both have jazz hands in our backgrounds, she as an actress, me as a West End stage kid. But there's a ten-year age gap between our boyfriends and they're as different to each other as we are similar, so double dating isn't really on the cards.

Of course, there are moments when I struggle with envy when I encounter really tight groups of friends. On social media, it can seem like everyone else's year is divided up into regular red-letter days with their crew. From the outside, it really does look like a lot of fun. Meanwhile, I haven't had to RSVP to a single wedding in at least three years, which isn't such a tragedy, because I find hen parties extraordinarily hard work. But still, you can't help feeling a little left out.

Nothing says B-list friend more than a wedding day NFI.

Those pangs were never felt more keenly than when I had a baby. Because my boyfriend is younger than me and my confidantes are either his age and not ready for a family, still single, living thousands of miles away or else have chosen to be child-free, I didn't have anyone to share the 'journey' with. Say what you like about 'old friends', there's no doubt that sticking with a gang, especially those in couples, who hit life milestones around the same time really pays off when it comes to motherhood. My first year of being a mum was brutally isolating and really made me re-evaluate my network.

So, for the first time in a really long time, I started spending time with groups of women, all of us with young children. After all, motherhood is another milestone when you're meant to gather a new pack of pals. But instead of feeling buoyed up and excited about our scheduled meetings and diary dates, I soon began to dread them. It took hardly any time at all to scratch the surface and find that the idea of a squad, for me at least, is far more appealing than the reality.

The truth is that I'm a true urbanite and love the anonymity of the city, so the lack of personal business and the associated gossip in a group is a massive turn-off. Very soon it can feel like you're in an episode of *The Hills*. Obviously, not everyone in a gang can be equally enamoured with each other, and before long it becomes apparent that, actually, Sophie can barely stand Jane, but they have to hang out with each other every bloody weekend for the sake of 'the group'. It's also cripplingly expensive to keep up with all the activities and starts to really cut into your free time . . . and by that, yes, I do mean Netflix hours.

And so I began to embrace the idea that my social set-up was as much about my preferences as my circumstances. At a certain point you do have to look in the mirror and recognize the common denominator staring back is you. Instead of desperately needing to be part of the group, turns out I've actually always wanted to be left out, I just hadn't noticed. Where some people thrive in a gang, I wither inside because I need the intimacy of one-on-one girlfriendships rather than the support of a pack. I didn't need a posse of mum friends, I realized, I just needed one. And nearly two years of courtship later, I've found her – Anne Marie, who I met on social media while our babies were putting us both through the reflux wringer – a new star to add to the constellation of women in my life.

Of course, that doesn't mean that my version of what friendship looks like is without its drawbacks, or that it would suit everyone. But what I've come to understand is that it's tailor-made for my personality, rather than conforming to what it's 'supposed' to look like. I like the way I can share

WHERE SOME PEOPLE THRIVE IN A GANG, I WITHER INSIDE BECAUSE I NEED THE INTIMACY OF ONE-ON-ONE GIRLFRIENDSHIPS RATHER THAN THE SUPPORT OF A PACK. I DIDN'T NEED A POSSE OF MUM FRIENDS, I REALIZED, I JUST NEEDED ONE.

my problems individually with my close friends and they don't talk about them among themselves. I value the very different perspectives they offer me. Conversely, I would bristle at the idea of friends dissecting my personal life together behind my back and serving up collective advice.

Truthfully, the idea of anything associated with a pack mentality – matching T-shirts, endless in-jokes, annual group pics, WhatsApp groups, festivals (the horror), Doodle calendars – makes me feel overwhelmed, probably because whenever I've been rolling deep I ended up turning into a people-pleaser and spent my time and money on things I wasn't interested in because I felt honour-bound to do so. Honestly, I don't ever want to go to nine weddings over one summer again. Having a group of friends once seemed like the end goal but, actually, making relationships with individuals who may or may not get on with each other has served me far better.

All relationships happen behind closed doors anyway. Those BFFs smiling so genuinely on Insta might be more *Mean Girls* than *Stand by Me*. You just can't tell. Beth and I have a deeply romantic relationship, even though we've never lived closer than 3,500 miles from each other. We message and Facetime every day, from 9 a.m. EST, and have carried each other through life, death and everything in between. Our bond might sound surprising considering the distance, but despite becoming close when we were both travelling the world with expense accounts, we're still thick as thieves today (even though the rock 'n' roll has bubbled down to a simmer).

Idolizing the model of 'five best friends who met in Year 7 and have since shared every single step of their lives together' does a disservice to all the other brilliant friend formats like ours. It suggests there is only one way to give and receive friendship, and that involves holding on to mates who are there by dint of no more than longevity. If we take the adage that friends are there for a season, a reason or a lifetime, how many of us are holding on to people for a lifetime when their season has long passed? We all know it's better to be single than in a bad marriage. I'd argue it's also better to be friend*less* than stuck with bad friends, especially if you're only 'friends' because your parents know each other.

So, if you're not in a mythical group hanging out in a coffee shop/dive bar/countryside church en route to yet another marquee, stop feeling like you're missing out. Instead, let's celebrate our Facetime friends, long-distance besties and tête-à-tête chums instead. My petite non-squad might never be turned into an aspirational sitcom or chick flick, but it's full of supportive, eccentric, clever women who tick more of my boxes than any man I've ever dated. And it's the only one I've ever managed to feel at home in. That, surely, is the true definition of #friendshipgoals.

YOMI ADEGOKE AND ELIZABETH UVIEBINENÉ

How to build a business without breaking a friendship

Elizabeth and Yomi are the co-authors of Slay in Your Lane, *the multi-award-winning guide to life for black women. After meeting at Warwick University, the pair pursued careers in marketing and journalism respectively, before generating a nine-way auction for their ground-breaking book. Sparking a national conversation about the unique challenges faced by black women, the book was called 'brilliant' by London's Mayor, Sadiq Khan. Elizabeth is currently business culture columnist for the* Financial Times, *while Yomi is a columnist at the* i *newspaper and women's columnist at the* Guardian.

~~~~~~~~~

A strong friendship is like magic. You can't see it, but it can do incredible things. For us, it's been like a superpower, amping up our courage and strength ever since we first met as freshers at the University of Warwick.

Over the years, our friendship has empowered us to show everyone else who we are, and what we can do, too. And now our friendship has conjured up something more incredible than we could ever imagine – a business. A brand. A movement. People often ask if working together has made us closer or created more arguments, and we always answer to both – honestly, no. But that's not to say it's easy, or that friendship is a secret weapon for professional success. In many ways, the stakes of working with a friend are far higher. Because if you're anything like us, in work as in life your friendship will be your foundation. So we wanted to share our tips with you for building a business without breaking a friendship. And like everything else we do, it's a joint effort. Two perspectives, one goal . . .

Yomi says:

1. DO YOU LOVE HER PROFESSIONALLY AS WELL AS PERSONALLY?

The only reason our book, *Slay in Your Lane*, exists is because Elizabeth rates me. She likes me, sure. After being best friends since our university days, I'd even go as far as to say she loves me. But when she rang asking me to write a book that would help her navigate the workplace as a black woman, these weren't the reasons she came to me. It was because she rates and respects my work as a writer. In turn, I asked her to co-write it with me because I rate and respect her marketing acumen. Often, when friends aren't supportive of our side hustles or new ventures, it's tempting to assume they are being vindictive or petty, but it's a line of thinking I have recently tried to challenge. Though I'll support friends regardless, I never want the entire basis of my friends' support to be out of obligation or guilt. I want them to engage with my work because they actually value what I'm doing and think I'm doing it well. Elizabeth involved me not because she had to but because she wanted to and thought I could do justice to something she wanted to see created. I thought the same about her. Even if we weren't friends, I would have wanted to learn from her professionally. Can you say the same about your friend?

2. BE HONEST ABOUT YOUR EGO

One of the things that first drew me to Elizabeth was her ability to be so confidently understated. In a world where the overriding economy is 'clicks' and 'clout', she's always been happy to do the less glamorous jobs – she's as happy pulling the curtains as she is to be centre stage. In fact, while we're both Beyoncés in our own right, neither of us

THOUGH I'LL SUPPORT FRIENDS REGARDLESS, I NEVER WANT THE ENTIRE BASIS OF MY FRIENDS' SUPPORT TO BE OUT OF OBLIGATION OR GUILT. I WANT THEM TO ENGAGE WITH MY WORK BECAUSE THEY ACTUALLY VALUE WHAT I'M DOING AND THINK I'M DOING IT WELL.

has ever shirked the Kelly or Michelle roles either. It's this that I believe makes us work so well together. We have been aware for a long time that the *Slay in Your Lane* movement stopped being about us individually as soon as we hung up on that fateful phone call. It's always been much bigger, which leaves little room for our own egos. If one of you craves the limelight more than the other, that's fine, but it's important that work is split in a way you're both comfortable with. And that can only be worked out through an honest conversation at the start – communication is key.

3. PROTECT YOUR TIME AS FRIENDS

When I first started in journalism I was almost militant about not wanting to mix business and pleasure. Fast-forward several years and, suddenly, my best friend Elizabeth, who had been one of my biggest forms of escape from the media industry, was not only working in it but doing so alongside me! Our daily two-hour phone calls about reality television and Tinder dates were now replaced almost entirely with finance chat and agendas for upcoming meetings. To be honest, I always say if I had written the book alone, as Elizabeth initially suggested, she would have been my plus-one to every industry event anyway! But in the early days I did begin to miss my best friend, even though I was spending more time with her than ever. This is why we created our 'Sunday summit' – a dedicated slot on Sundays at 12 p.m., when for about two hours we have all book- and brand-related conversations for the week ahead. We catch up on the previous week's events and set goals about what we want to achieve during the next, so that work chat doesn't have to crop up during our free time. Those boundaries mean we both work to a clear plan, but the important stuff – the even more important stuff – doesn't get hijacked either.

4. YOUR FRIENDSHIP IS YOUR FOUNDATION

Elizabeth and I were best friends before this book was released. It's often assumed that it will have changed our relationship, but in all honesty, it hasn't. We met at university and, just like other friends, we sometimes fall out. Whether it's to do with our personal or our professional lives, our approach is the same. Being old friends means we're less likely to dance around the truth and more comfortable being frank, so we'll discuss the issue at hand as soon as possible, ensuring it doesn't fester and grow by ignoring it. What we both know is that our friendship comes first in every way. To us, that means ensuring we are as okay as possible before we do anything in terms of work. The brand cannot exist without our friendship but, more importantly, we as individuals probably couldn't either.

5. DON'T ALWAYS SEE EYE TO EYE? GOOD!

Elizabeth and I are wildly different, but also very similar – we're likely to go into a shop, pick out the same item of clothing, and then style it so differently and distinctly you wouldn't even realize we're wearing the same thing. It's the same at work – we both have the same vision for Slay in Your Lane, we just sometimes see different routes to our end destination. In fact, being friends means we can capitalize on different viewpoints in a way regular business partners might not. We're not afraid to challenge each other. And because of our pre-existing trust and respect, we can agree to disagree or concede a point, even when it's a topic we might, technically, know more about, without any loss of pride.

Elizabeth says:

1. YOUR FRIENDSHIP IS NOT ENOUGH . . .

You both need to be equally passionate about the venture. There is nobody on this earth who will ever be more committed to the Slay in Your Lane brand than Yomi and I. Our joint obsession is often the fuel that keeps the Slay engine going, even when we experience setbacks and obstacles. Ask yourself, does your friend like the idea of working on a business with me *generally*, or are they passionate and personally invested in *this* business? The business and your friendship are two separate things. Independently of you, your friend needs to be inspired and motivated by the idea itself. When I pitched the idea of the book to Yomi, I knew it was a good idea, but I didn't have a personal investment beyond the fact that I wanted someone to write it so I could read it!

ASK YOURSELF, DOES YOUR FRIEND LIKE THE IDEA OF WORKING ON A BUSINESS WITH ME *GENERALLY*, OR ARE THEY PASSIONATE AND PERSONALLY INVESTED IN *THIS* BUSINESS? THE BUSINESS AND YOUR FRIENDSHIP ARE TWO SEPARATE THINGS.

When she pitched it back to me as a movement and a brand, that's when I became personally invested in working on it. I didn't even write a dissertation at university, so long-form writing wasn't something I naturally wanted to spend my free time doing! However, because I was passionate about the wider impact of the conversation we wanted to start, this ignited my passion.

2. YOU'RE FRIENDS, BUT ARE YOU ON THE SAME FREQUENCY?

Starting out in business, you both need to have an obsession with the vision. You have a limited amount of time between being filled with hot passion and the often harsh reality of getting the idea off the ground, so before committing money, resources or even energy to the idea, spend as much time as possible talking – about the bigger picture, not practicalities. Within a week of coming up with our concept, Yomi and I did nothing else but talk. As I was living in Yomi's family home at the time, we would wake up in next-door bedrooms, get ready for work and walk to the station together, all while discussing what we needed to make this dream of ours a reality. Then we'd get on the train and talk about it some more. We'd even phone over our lunch breaks and sometimes get the train home together so we could bounce more ideas around.

This is sound advice, generally, but especially important when going into business with a friend. Because, as best friends, you probably overestimate how in tune you are with each other. It's key to dispel any assumptions early on, so this is the time to ask questions like: If everything went our way, what would success look like? If things didn't go our way, what would make you walk away? Answering these questions ensures you're not only on the same page but on the same frequency.

After all, unlike other business partnerships, the stakes are far higher – your years of friendship.

3. ARE YOU IN THE SAME HEADSPACE?

When you're starting something from scratch, inevitably, your personal and professional lives will bleed into each other. But what feels like giving 110 per cent to one person can look very different to another. When Yomi and I first had the idea of SIYL, we were lucky: in our early twenties and our first proper jobs post university, we were both able to channel equal amounts of energy towards the book. We've made the same sacrifices too: we used to go out raving a lot, but over the last few years have had to swap our dresses and dancing shoes for early nights and dressing gowns! Being at a similar life stage can help set expectations, but more important is to be in the same headspace. If you have different commitments, say a full-time job or children, you each have to be realistic about what you can feasibly expect. This will require empathy and pragmatism on both sides, so create a spreadsheet and actually quantify it. Agree what progress on your idea would look like on a daily, weekly and monthly basis and split the work fairly, taking into account each other's prior commitments. This is the time to be transparent. And if there's any point in the future when you feel there's a mismatch in your efforts, refer back to the spreadsheet for perspective.

4. ARE YOU STRESS COMPATIBLE?

It's really important to understand how a friend handles pressure and stress before working together because – you guessed it – there will inevitably be lots of stress and lots of pressure! Yomi and I went to university together, so we had an insight into each other's working styles. Frankly, we've seen each other at our worst! But if you've only hung out socially, think about how they manage money, deal with an unexpected incident like a delayed flight, or their attitudes to tricky neighbours. As friends, how have you handled fallouts with each other in the past? If you have a friend who doesn't deal with stress in a way you can cope with or support, then it's probably a bad idea to embark on a business with them.

But if you do, it might be worth writing a friendship mission statement – a line, or two, that encapsulates your friendship and what you love about each other, to put things in perspective when you're both feeling stressed or morale is low. We didn't, but looking back, there were times it would have been helpful to have had something written down. When times are tough, it will boost empathy and remind you why, as best friends, you're the best people to build this business together.

5. MAKE YOUR FRIENDSHIP AN ASSET, NOT AN OBSTACLE

There can sometimes be a stigma about mixing business with pleasure, especially when it comes to pitching your business to outsiders. Yet when Yomi and I do panels, go on to podcasts and meet new people, the comment is always what a great rapport we have. Our friendship is actually a huge asset. Don't play it down or feel it makes your business any less credible, or that you have to create formal structures – unless you want to. I remember when we were being interviewed for live TV and, having never done that before, I was feeling really nervous. I will never forget how calm Yomi made me feel before we had to go on, because she knew instinctively how to put me at ease. Equally, I knew that, whatever happened, even if I froze, she would have my back. So never see your friendship as an obstacle. In so many ways, our friendship has given us both the confidence to do things we never thought possible.

SHAPPI KHORSANDI

Everything I've learned from being a flaky friend

Shappi Khorsandi was born in Iran, but her family was forced to flee to London following the publication of a satirical poem by her father. One of the UK's finest comedians, she has appeared on countless TV shows, including **Have I Got News For You, Mock the Week, Live at the Apollo** *and* **Michael McIntyre's Comedy Roadshow.** *In 2017, based on her love of camping at Glastonbury, she took part in* **I'm a Celebrity . . . Get Me Out of Here,** *leaving first, with ten thousand ant bites. She has twice been a panellist on* **Question Time,** *holds an honorary doctorate from the University of Winchester, and is vice-president of Humanists UK. Shappi has also written two books – the bestselling memoir* **A Beginner's Guide to Acting English** *(2009) and a novel,* **Nina is Not OK** *(2016).*

My name is Shappi, and I am a flaky friend. Well, I used to be. I am a recovering flake, and getting better every day. Over the years I have done terribly flaky things with cringing regularity, from gateway behaviours of leaving calls or texts unanswered for far too long to the more destructive habit of cancelling at the eleventh hour because something 'better' came up. I have even – and this is really, really bad – been a last-minute wedding no-show. A wedding in France, that is, with all the expense and organizational headaches for the happy couple that entails. Yes, I *know*.

And yet, while I'm not proud of my flaky past, in a weird kind of way I'm grateful for it. Now I have largely moved on from that phase, I can look back and see the valuable lessons being a flake taught me about myself. I also like to think it makes me much more compassionate towards friends who flake on me, too.

Because one thing I'm sure of is that flaky friends generally aren't bad people. Take that wedding in France. The reality was I was moving house the day before, I had no childcare for my toddler and was in the midst of a very stressful divorce. Naturally, if I had told the couple even a few weeks before, explained how tricky the logistics were looking, they would have understood. They would also have been able to give that hotel room and precious place on the minibus to someone else. But I felt terrified of seeming disorganized, or like I didn't value them enough. And so I RSVP'd yes, then stressed about it, stewed on it, and left it until two days before to admit that I wasn't actually going. I felt awful about it for years. And, funnily enough, we're not exactly in touch any more. But you see, very often with flakes, we say yes to things we can't possibly manage for fear of letting people down. Then of course we *can't* manage it and so let everyone down. It is stressful being an unreliable person, let me tell you.

With a flaky friend you soon learn that 'Yes! Definitely!' means 'Let's see what happens on the night, shall we?' Sooner or later, you have a decision to make: accept it, ditch them, or – the least British option – talk about it. My official best friend took the latter. I have known her since I was seven; she is the most reliable person I know and also exceptionally kind-hearted. She let me live in her one-bedroom flat while I was skint and doing open spots on the comedy circuit, and never in her life has she committed to anything she could not stand by. She is, in short, the yin to my yang. In my twenties I was very excitable and rambunctious. I loved meeting new people to have fun with and I ran around a lot, being very unpredictable and unreliable. In my need to be liked, I'd say yes to pretty much every invitation and never had a prayer of honouring even half. A classic flake.

One night, I came home from the cinema and my best friend sat me down. 'Do you remember saying you'd go and see that film tomorrow night with *me*?' she asked. Umm, yes, I did. 'But then you made a new friend and went with her tonight, and now I have no one to go with.' Those were the facts. I could not deny it.

She wasn't telling me off, she was literally explaining my behaviour to me, as if to a child. 'I always know that when you arrange something with me I'm your Plan B,' she continued. 'It's not a nice way to feel.' I was mortified. There wasn't a person I respected more in the world, but here she was, telling me I'd disrespected *her* by being a massive flake.

As I reflected on her words, I realized I'd never thought that I mattered as much to her as she did to me. The reality is, flakes often don't have very high self-esteem. It's not that I didn't consider her feelings, I didn't consider that I mattered enough to her to make an impact on her feelings. Do you see how I've managed to make myself the victim here? You may be thinking 'classic flake move', but there is my truth. I am forever grateful for my friend's honesty. She could have just ditched me. But she is a fountain of love and understanding. When you tell a friend they are a flake, what you're actually saying is that they matter to you, and when she saw my behaviour change I was forgiven. I've never let her down since.

Of course, here we must make the distinction between a 'flake' and someone who is simply not very nice and a 'taker' who never gives back. I have had quite a few friends like this, too. It took me long into my thirties to realize that just because someone makes me laugh and is a ridiculous amount of fun on a night out, it doesn't necessarily make them a good friend. It's fair to say that I used to be very needy (and, let's face it, no one becomes a stand-up comedian because they have

**WHEN YOU TELL
A FRIEND THEY ARE
A FLAKE, WHAT
YOU'RE ACTUALLY
SAYING IS THAT THEY
MATTER TO YOU.**

a *surplus* of self-worth), so for a long time I allowed myself to be drawn into toxic friendships with gregarious people where I was treated more like a sidekick than a mate. Bullies, really. A girl at uni once pushed me fully clothed into a swimming pool on holiday in front of some boys we were flirting with. So let's be clear – toxic is not the same as flaky. When someone thinks humiliating you is funny, or constantly letting you down is no biggie, push them out of your life.

But if your flaky friend is essentially a good person, talk to them. I braved this myself with a neighbour I became close with shortly after I'd become a single mum. After happily hanging out for a while, she started cancelling on me – texting at the last minute to cancel a dinner date at my house. Technology, of course, makes flaking far too easy. (My advice if you do not consider yourself a flake is to always call. No one appreciates a cold text cancelling a fun plan.)

When I received the third cancellation in a row I decided to tell her how I felt. Which was essentially: 'I'm lonely now that it's just me and the baby, so when I make an arrangement, it means something to me. I look forward to *you*.'

Her response was equally truthful. She'd been cancelling because she was in a bad place. She felt depressed and kept making plans that, when it came down to it, she just couldn't keep. Now *that*, I related to. Saying yes to things out of obligation, not feeling you can be honest and say, 'I'm low, I don't want company,' is a trap that many flakes fall into. With all our cards on the table, my neighbour and I were able to remain friends.

For the 'flaker', you have to trust that true friendship can differentiate between 'flaky' and a life which is so full to the brim that you can't take on any more. This January, an old friend and her family were due to come to mine for Sunday lunch. It was the last weekend of what had been a tricky

Christmas time for me. A work deadline, a relationship split, a chest infection . . . by the time our date rolled around, I just didn't have the energy. We had arranged the lunch weeks back, but now I was in desperate need of a day padding about my house in a dressing gown doing nothing. So what did I do? I cancelled an hour before they were due to leave their house. But because I am no longer a total flake and because I now only keep people in my life who are kind and sweet and loving, I called her up and explained exactly what was going on for me. She was full of understanding and we rearranged – and stuck to – a new date.

Over the years, I've also come to believe that flakiness can be cured. And often, that it's time that is the healer. Anna was one of my favourite people to hang out with at university. She was fun, funny and a massive flake. It hurt my feelings. I didn't understand it. We really connected and had such a great time together, but it always felt like I was the friend she could drop at a moment's notice.

After university, we stayed in touch, but months would go by before she returned a call. When she did, we would talk for hours, laughing until we couldn't breathe. She loved to go travelling and raving back in the nineties while I was carving out a career in stand-up comedy, so with hindsight, I can see that at that stage we were simply incompatible. At the time, though, I was much more invested in the friendship than she was. In fact, looking back, I was needy and quite demanding. I didn't know it then, but it's important to check your own expectations of friendship too. Self-soothing is a life skill and you can't call a friend 'flaky' just because they can't drop everything every time you're feeling insecure.

Still, I had my baby boy and Anna all but disappeared. I'd see her posts on Facebook, always partying, always travelling, and I gave up writing to her or arranging to meet. Five years went

**SELF-SOOTHING IS A
LIFE SKILL AND YOU
CAN'T CALL A FRIEND
'FLAKY' JUST BECAUSE
THEY CAN'T DROP
EVERYTHING EVERY
TIME YOU'RE FEELING
INSECURE.**

by, by which time I was pregnant with my second child. Then out of the blue she sent me a 'Hey babe!' chatty message, excitedly telling me she was pregnant too, had moved to my locale, and wasn't this going to be brilliant because we could hang out all the time and do baby stuff together? She said she hadn't been in touch before because she'd been 'crazy busy' and that she was so pleased to be back in touch with me, her 'soul sister'.

But I couldn't just click back into our old dynamic. I was almost forty and no longer that needy twenty-something who would jump whenever she called. I had also weathered a bitter, drawn-out divorce and been shown what true friendship was by those who carried me through it.

I wrote back and congratulated her. But then I also told her that Obama (who was president at the time) was 'crazy busy', not her, or me, adding that 'We make time for the people we want to make time for. My son is five, you haven't even met him. A friendship like this isn't one I want to pick up again.'

A few months later, both heavily pregnant, we saw each other at a mutual friend's fortieth. We hugged, we cried, we talked and she told me what had *really* been going on for her during those long absences. She, too, had been going through a whole load of *life*. It just hadn't been the time for our friendship to blossom. Now, more in synch, our six-year-old girls are the best of pals and our friendship has become one of the warmest and most enriching I have.

You see, sometimes you have to trust that a friend who is distracted by other things in their life still cares about you but their journey has taken them in another direction for a while. Sure, if someone consistently lets me down, and things don't get better, I now have no qualms just to let it fizzle out. Equally, sometimes you have to accept that your flaky friend is just not into you.

But I also believe that, overall, the friends who can be there for you are, and those who aren't simply can't. Two weeks ago, while we were washing up, Anna said how sorry she was that she wasn't there for me during my divorce, ten years ago. 'I did know what was going on,' she admitted. 'I just stayed away.' She had her reasons – as did I, before that wedding.

Now, in my mid-forties, I know who makes me feel good and who the irreparable flakes are. If I can't commit to something, I try to own it, rather than slinking away at the last minute. And when a friend is a bit flaky, I tend to assume they have a lot on. I don't always make it about me, like I used to. But my recovery is a work-in-progress. It's not perfect. Just last week I cancelled a trip to see a dance show with a friend at the last moment. I was honest and told her I wanted to take my daughter instead. Happily, Anna understood.

HELEN BOWNASS

The onscreen friendships that changed my life

Helen Bownass has been entertainment director at Stylist *magazine since 2014, a job she didn't even know how to dream about when growing up in Portsmouth. As well as interviewing celebrities like Oprah Winfrey, Hillary Clinton and Reese Witherspoon, she oversees Under Her Eye, a unique initiative that reviews films through a female lens, and curates* Stylist's *annual Remarkable Women awards. A life-long joiner-inner, Helen is a loyal member of both a book group and a netball team, the aptly named Cool Runnings, where she plays a highly enthusiastic goal defence.*

~~~~~~~~~~

When I was ten, my parents took my sister and me to Orlando. I'd never ever been on a plane before, so my excitement levels were high, verging on hysterical. But about two days in I dug out The Baby-Sitters Club books from a suitcase. From that point on, all I wanted to do was sit in the hotel room devouring stories of a group of girlfriends who had amazing adventures – and the best snacks. Screw you, Mickey!

I'm slightly ashamed to admit that wasn't atypical behaviour. While my friends were obsessed with tales of horses or ballet dancers, I just wanted to know about how girls, and later women, talked to and acted around each other. When I read the Famous Five books I skipped through any bit that wasn't George or Anne speaking (and, as they were written in the 1940s, they didn't get to speak much). As I moved through school and university, that compulsion showed no signs of abating – why would I want to watch films or TV shows about aliens or criminals, when *Clueless* existed?

So when *Sex and the City* came out, I felt like all my pop-culture prayers had been answered. And like every other woman glued to that series, I spent huge swathes of time discussing which character I was (Carrie, like the big journalist cliché I am) and who my friends would be in our parallel New York world.

It's only been recently, as I've begun to reflect more on my fascination with observing fictional friendships (fuelled, I suspect, by my forever need to fit in and have people like me), that I can recognize that some of those friendships I was consuming weren't authentic. And, actually, that they may have in fact stoked my fears.

Sex and the City, for example, doesn't represent friendship as I now know it, as a late thirty-something-year-old woman. Carrie et al. had the best time together, but the show is really more about how they relate within the framework of male attention, rather than an exploration of the pulsating, difficult, shifting bond between women. It fetishizes friendship without truly exploring its light and shade.

What *SATC* did do, though, was lead a renewed and much needed charge for centring female friendship on TV. It took a while but, for the first time in my career, women and their friendships are increasingly the subject of some of the most critically acclaimed *and* populist TV shows, from *Girls* to *Big Little Lies*. It's become particularly prominent on the big screen, too. When I was growing up, studies in male friendship weren't just popular film fodder, they had their own entire genre: the male buddy movie. Meanwhile, female relationships in film were largely represented as one of two tropes: woman pitted against woman to get a job/man/pair of shoes, or psychotic. Now, young women are growing up with films like

Booksmart and *Girls Trip*, which are authentic, representative and intimate, showing female friendship in all its multifaceted glory. I can't imagine how my view of the world – and myself – might have shifted if I'd had those offerings to observe.

That said, all those representations of friendship – both good and toxic – taught me valuable lessons about that vital bond, and shaped my own attitude to – and expectations of – friendship. Even though some of the characters would never be welcome to share a bottle of Malbec with me, here are the five pairings that have had the biggest impact on my life . . .

GIRLS JUST WANT TO HAVE FUN (1985)

There was a period of my life at the tail end of the eighties that I rented *Girls Just Want to Have Fun* every weekend from the Blockbuster Video shop on my local high street. One Saturday, my dad came back with *K-9* instead. I still remember that little pan of anger boiling over in my stomach when he presented it to me. I refused to watch it, and I don't blame me. Who would want to sit through a film about a police dog when they could watch Sarah Jessica Parker, a student at a strict Catholic school, defy her father and enter a TV dance competition?

The dance montages – and there were many – were to die for, but what I was really obsessed by was the dynamic between Janey (SJP) and Lynne (played by Helen Hunt). Lynne was daring, sassy (back then, I had no idea how to be sassy, but seeing her whip off her school skirt on the bus and turn it inside out so it became a leather skirt gave me a good idea) and confident about what she and Janey should do with their lives. Everything I wasn't.

I couldn't relate to the outfits or all the hair, despite the fact I was also living in that exact decade, but for someone who attended a very strict Catholic school herself, *Girls Just Want to Have Fun* was a timely reminder that a good friendship can be liberating and that, occasionally, we all need someone to help us embrace our rebellious streak and to worry slightly less about always doing the right thing. Even if that involves inciting hundreds of punks to crash the birthday party of your mortal enemy.

BROAD CITY (2014–19)

Although my friends have never smuggled my faeces out of my flat in a box because I've got a lover over and can't get the toilet to flush, I am convinced they would if I asked (I wouldn't, I promise). That said, until *Broad City* put the idea in my head, I never knew how important it was to celebrate the messy, unpolished side of friendship this scenario surely falls into. The brilliant sitcom, written by and starring Abbi Jacobson and Ilana

Glazer, is about two women living in New York, and centres entirely on their friendship in all its ridiculous, scrappy, life-changing glory, rather than either of the protagonists' search for a partner. That was – and still is – radical.

Besides celebrating every bodily function, what I ultimately took from *Broad City* was a reminder to give praise to our friendships and the unconditional love wrapped up in them. Abbi and Ilana taught me that we don't need to hide any side of ourselves from the people who truly love us. Platonic relationships are often quieter and less dramatic than romantic ones; they're a self-sufficient cactus, to romance's windowsill of needy succulents. That's often a big part of their appeal – they don't need managing. But that doesn't mean that bond, and those people, are any less precious or deserving of celebration. Abbi and Ilana are the kweens of this: they celebrate their anniversary, they go on madcap adventures together and they always lift each other up and celebrate each other's magic. As Ilana memorably put it: 'Your ass looks incredible . . . Your head and body, too. But we all know who's the star of the show here.'

INSECURE (2016–PRESENT)

My best friend is supportive, brave and – if needed – unafraid to give me hard truths about my life decisions – or my lack of decision. From 'never get that haircut again' to 'I'm sorry, babe, but it's time to get over him now,' those words always come from a place of love and wanting me to live my happiest life. But she's also the only one who will call me out on my bullshit and make me face a reality I'm burying my head in the sand to avoid.

I'd always been a little nervous of hearing it until I watched the first three seasons of *Insecure*, created by and starring Issa Rae. The comedy about a woman, Issa, navigating modern life with her best friend, Molly (Yvonne Orji), shows them holding each other accountable and facing difficult truths together – rather than weaponizing their insecurities against each other, which we so often see onscreen. Whether it's pointing out that hanging out with an ex you have unresolved feelings for is destructive, confronting the other's intimacy issues, or suggesting they could do with some therapy, they do it in a way that is kind and authentic. Molly and Issa even have a codeword (Malibu) which is used to denote that everything that's about to be said is utterly unfiltered. And the power of this being an authentic and specific friendship between two black women can't be underestimated either – for them, their friendship offers an extra layer of comfort, being a place they don't have to hide any part of themselves.

My best friend always tells me she knows me better than I know myself, and watching *Insecure* made me realize that she's probably right. And it made me face up to an inescapable truth – that having women in my life who want the best for me, no matter how hard it is to hear sometimes, is invaluable.

FLEABAG (2016–19)

If you believed everything social media tells you, your sister is your absolute best friend. The other half of you. The greatest human you've ever met. Which is nice for those for whom that's true, but for everyone else it's another tool to beat ourselves up with. I once caught myself thinking: 'Am I weird because I think my sister is brilliant, but not my soulmate?' As if juggling full-on careers and personal lives and geography wasn't already tricky enough. But *Fleabag* paints a picture of sisterhood and friendship that made me feel a bit more like a functioning human.

When the series starts, it's Fleabag's relationship with her best friend – who she inadvertently caused the death of, after sleeping with her boyfriend – that's at the heart of the narrative. But over time we realize that the real love story at the centre of *Fleabag* is between her and her sister, Claire. Throughout both series, they straddle a wisp-thin line between disdain and delight in each other. Theirs is a very relatable relationship – they can make each other angrier than any other human on the planet, don't have a lot in common and despair at how the other chooses to live their life. At one point, Claire says: 'We're not friends. We are sisters. Find your own friends.' In saying this, she's both right and wrong – and, refreshingly, we are allowed to be on both sides of the argument.

But what *Fleabag* shows so beautifully is that, when it's really important – say, pretending that you're having a miscarriage to cover up the fact your sister really is, agreeing a haircut looks French when actually it looks like a pencil, or giving your broken sister the courage to leave a toxic, abusive, alcoholic husband – Fleabag and Claire are all in. They've got each other's back. It's a vital bit of reassurance, so rarely given, that it doesn't matter that you spend 50 per cent of your time fantasizing about pushing your sister's face in their birthday cake, because they're also the only person you'd run through an airport for.

FRANCES HA (2012)

Before working as director on *Lady Bird* and *Little Women* – both utterly excellent examples of the female experience – Greta Gerwig also starred in films. *Frances Ha* is my stand-out. It's the story of Frances, a dancer, and her best friend and flatmate, Sophie: 'We're the same person with different hair,' they're fond of saying, until they're not . . . Sophie moves on and in with her boyfriend and Frances laments that she's treating her 'like a three-hour brunch friend'.

Seeing Frances flail and cling on to her friend and their in-jokes hit me deep in my gut. Who hasn't felt that nauseous lurch when a dear friend falls in love and moves away from you? And if you're Frances (me), you've probably behaved rather badly as you failed to deal with it. But there was an extra kick as I watched this and realized I've also been that friend on the other side, too, and probably not behaved as sensitively as I should when in a relationship.

Thank god this film exists, though. It made me feel less alone to know I'm not a totally dysfunctional arsehole just because I wish life could sometimes stay the same, and that no one had to move on. And reminded me that friendships do change, but that evolution isn't a bad thing, it's just a different thing. It's important, too, to see loneliness onscreen. While friendship is lifeblood, it's also not something everyone is lucky enough to experience, or not always in the way we want to. We all need a reminder of how fortunate we are when we find it.

GINA MARTIN

When you love your friends but don't like their opinions

Having campaigned tirelessly following her own assault, activist Gina Martin is best known for changing the law and making upskirting (taking a sexually intrusive photograph up someone's skirt) illegal. A former advertising copywriter, she is now an ambassador for UN Women UK and advocates for regular people creating change. Her first book, Be the Change, *is a practical guide for activists starting out. Gina was recently named one of the* Evening Standard's 1,000 most influential people in London, *and one of* Time *magazine's #100 Next Influential People.*

I'm sitting cross-legged on the floor of my apartment in London, with Rey, one of my closest friends, my partner, Jordy, and good friend Zoe. It's August 2017 – my twenty-sixth birthday – and we're having a takeaway because I'm not that up for celebrating. 'So,' I tell them anxiously, 'the producer says her angle for tomorrow's interview is, "If you don't want photos taken of your vagina, wear trousers."'

A month before, while I was at a festival in London's Hyde Park, a group of guys stuck their hands between my legs, took photos of my crotch and shared them around to 'teach me a lesson' for rebuffing their advances. After snatching the phone and handing it – along with the guy – into the police, I learned that taking non-consensual upskirt images wasn't a sexual offence. So, alongside my full-time job, I launched a campaign to change the law, and had been working night and day to raise awareness ever since.

Rey shakes his head and takes a thoughtful sip of beer. 'Well, if the producer has a problem with that,' he says calmly, 'she can bring it up with the police, not a sexual-assault victim. You'll be fine. Just stick to your guns. And try to forget you're on live TV.'

As he's talking, I realize the real reason I've invited my friends round isn't because it's my birthday, but because I'm terrified. I'm scared of going on live TV to debate why this should be illegal because I'm so frustrated that it's even a debate. I need guidance from the people who know me best.

Rey really shows up for me in this conversation. He sits and listens and gives great advice. As does Zoe, who hands me a card as she leaves. 'I always knew you'd do wonderful things,' she's written inside. 'I love you, my friend.'

After the TV interview, I can tell everything is going to change. And I'm right – the next seventeen months are like being in a washing machine. I do countless news appearances. I approach law firms, and partner with a young, passionate lawyer called Ryan Whelan. We are in and out of Parliament constantly, learning about political procedure and meeting politicians. And I deal with rape threats online for a year. I cry more times than I can count. I barely hold down my job.

As I say, I knew then that everything was going to change. I just didn't realize that included some of my friendships.

Before the campaign, I had a core group of friends who were my go-tos, including Rey, who I met at a festival when I was an unsure twenty-year-old; Zoe, my most emotionally eloquent friend; Nicole, who suffers no fools; plus, of course, Jordy and my big sister, Stevie. Outside of that were half a dozen mates from uni who I'd catch up with over a drink but saw less often. None of us really talked about politics. Our conversations were built on funny stories from our past or the struggles of trying to carve out a career in London.

But during the start of my campaigning something slowly and steadily developed in me, namely, my understanding of the structural inequalities of society. Every day I met new people – campaigners fighting for human rights, investigative journalists with fascinating stories, NGOs seeking justice. With this came a whole new level of education that I'd never had before. My world grew, my understanding ballooned, and I guess you could say some of my reference points shifted.

I soon noticed that not all my friends were on my new wavelength. This wasn't a big revelation; there was no dramatic falling-out, no one cried. Instead, I felt an imperceptible shift in certain friendships that crept in over time. We'd be sitting in our local beer garden and something like the refugee crisis would come up – an inescapable news story at the time. I'd share an insight from a campaigner I'd recently worked with, but rather than being met with curiosity or questions, an awkward pause would follow, then a frown, or a sigh, before a very deliberate swerve back to the previous topic. It began to feel like I'd brought along a new friend who some people didn't want there.

On one particular night, during a critical stage of the campaign, I had exciting news to share. Explaining how much I wanted the government's official backing, I grinned as I told my friends I'd finally been granted crucial meetings with Conservative MPs. Almost everyone expressed support, but one friend accosted me later. 'Why on earth are you working with the Tories?' they demanded, with genuine dismay. I started to explain – changing things meant working with whoever was in power – but rather than listening, they dismissed me by ordering another drink. I felt embarrassed and deflated. How was it that this person, who knew me so well, didn't have any faith in my decisions? When you're young, you often prioritize being liked over doing or saying what's right. Or at least I did. But as you reach your late twenties and start to understand the world more, and your role in it, these points of principle become more important – and potentially divisive. It stung to hear they thought I was so wrong.

The truth is, I'm someone who thinks pretty deeply about the world, but very lightly about myself. Sit me in the pub and I'd rather debate the intricacies of what makes the perfect dog than preach social justice. But in my new role as an activist, when I go for a glass of wine with mates, as well as poring over some gossip about an old uni friend's life, I also want the conversations to reflect *my* life, too. Like we all do. If you work in an office, you discuss the trials and tribulations of that. If you work in campaigning, you want to discuss that, too. And man, is there stuff to discuss.

Around this time, I reconnected with Charlie, one of my oldest mates from school, and invited her to mine for some wine. We talked about the twelve years of friendship we'd missed, discovered we still had similar views now we were adults, and decided to meet up regularly. Each week we went to a bar and talked all things feminism with her lovely friend Julia. Those catch-ups were like therapy for me, and the first moment I realized I could curate a new community to fit my new life.

On 12 February 2019, after Ryan and I had lobbied the government for a year, the law was changed and upskirting was made a sexual offence. Amid the exhaustion and elation, it struck me that while I'd been organizing the campaign, managing a full-time job and regularly being trolled, a good friend I'd had for almost a decade hadn't once meaningfully checked how I was. It wasn't that we hadn't been in touch – we had. But instead of an 'are you okay?', they'd always wanted to start a debate, asking my opinion on something topical. And rather than value my insights from my work, this one friend I'd always thought respected me couldn't help but try and 'beat me' in every conversation, despite having literally no experience of the issue at hand. It was as if they were uncomfortable that I knew about something they didn't. After countless conversations like this, I felt completely deflated. 'Look,' I said firmly. 'We can't talk about this stuff. We just don't see eye to eye any more.'

When I look back, I can see that it would have been easier to deal with these differences with my friends if I had been in a more comfortable place myself. But I'd spent so much time in rooms with people who thought I cared 'too much'. The online abuse I received was peppered with eye-rolling accusations of me being a 'social justice warrior', a 'sensitive snowflake' or, best of all, 'a whiny little bitch'. When you're pushing for something new, so many conversations make you feel like the problem. And when those conversations occurred on a scruffy sofa with my very own friends, they were hard to take. That was one of the places this *wasn't meant to happen.*

I looked inwards a lot and worried that I was becoming unlikeable. But after a while I realized that those friends who had been a part of my everyday life during the campaign – who had seen the reality of it – got it. To Rey, Zoe, Nicole, Jordy and others, my opinions weren't annoying, because they'd seen them form. They'd been part of that journey and acclimatized with me. Those I didn't see as frequently were less invested. It wasn't that they didn't care, but to them my opinions were new and they saw this mad experience as something that had happened *to* me, not something I was the heartbeat of. They really only saw the Facebook posts begging people to share my petition. They flicked through the *Evening Standard* and saw their mate smiling triumphantly, so they WhatsApped a photo of it to me. They didn't see the grinding frustration or the sheer exhaustion. And when I retraced my steps I had to admit that I hadn't taken them all with me – my social life had, understandably, taken a backseat. Of course, I am entitled to talk about the things that matter to me, and to expect my friends to listen, as I would for them. But when I eventually turned up with all these new ideas, my friends had been landed with a slightly different friend, and therefore a slightly different friendship, that they hadn't asked for.

That's the challenge with long-term friendships – it's naive to expect you'll all grow in the same direction. As you move through your twenties, your friendships *will* change, whether you're changing a law or changing nappies. It's no longer enough to be friends through circumstance

AS YOU MOVE THROUGH YOUR TWENTIES, YOUR FRIENDSHIPS *WILL* CHANGE, WHETHER YOU'RE CHANGING A LAW OR CHANGING NAPPIES. IT'S NO LONGER ENOUGH TO BE FRIENDS THROUGH CIRCUMSTANCE, OR HAVING A SCHOOL UNIFORM OR A STREET IN COMMON.

or having a school uniform or a street in common. The older you get, the more you start to prioritize the friendships that align with your beliefs more closely. And as my friendships started to shift I noticed that many of those now expressing different opinions to me hadn't really been people I'd discussed my innermost feelings with. Yes, we'd been friends for a long time, but they were fun catch-up friends, so why did I have such high expectations? It's taken me until now to realize that this wasn't all on them. My needs had changed, too.

Faced with differences like this, I know some people are tempted to start over. To leave old friends behind. And yes, in certain circumstances, it has been healthy for me to do that, too. That friend who always wanted to debate with me? I haven't seen them since, and fully intended that to be the case when I called time on our conversations. Because while it's okay to have friends with different opinions, it's only okay if the respect is still there – and I didn't feel it was. I still care about them, of course. But I set a strong boundary and I'm proud of myself for it.

But generally, I had no desire to hit refresh. These people made me who I was; instead of replacing them, I just needed to add new perspectives to my support group. Perhaps, this way, I'd be able to show up in my older friendships as the old me more often? I pushed myself to make new connections. I met Sam, an actress and feminist comedian, and Kasey and Ben, who worked in gender inequality, and after that I didn't need to force all my friends to 'get it', because I felt validated elsewhere. I also made a personal rule to avoid discussing societal issues with certain friends. I rationalized this as giving myself time to mentally 'let go' of being an activist and just be Gina. Initially, it felt like a failure to have no-go areas, but that's the thing with people you really care about – you have to know when to let some comments go. And take it from me: whether your opinions differ on politics, parenting, or veganism (every friendship group will jar over *something*), having a drunken debate is never a good idea.

And as for those old friends who occasionally have different opinions to me? Well, they still can't be beaten when it comes to bringing cold, hard clarity to a problem. They can see past the determination I'm known for in my work and speak to the core me. Recently, I confessed to a uni friend that I was feeling overwhelmed by the many messages I receive detailing stories of abuse or asking for help. 'You always take on everyone's worries,' came the immediate response. 'You need to realize you can't change everything yourself.' They may not all be discussing internalized misogyny or white privilege with me yet, but they remind me of who I am when I feel like I'm floating in media madness and help me switch off by

**TAKE IT FROM ME:
WHETHER YOUR
OPINIONS DIFFER ON
POLITICS, PARENTING,
OR VEGANISM, HAVING
A DRUNKEN DEBATE IS
NEVER A GOOD IDEA.**

discussing something completely unrelated. And they do it because they care about me.

Not all your mates will see things the same as you, but then they don't all see you the same way either. And, actually, that makes brilliant and perfect sense. So if on my next birthday I need guidance from the people who know me best, I'll know there are lots of them I can call on. Their opinions might differ, and they might know different sides of me, but together they're what makes me whole.

HENRIETTA RIX AND ORLAGH MCCLOSKEY

Friendship unfiltered: two best friends, fifteen questions

Henrietta Rix and Orlagh McCloskey are the creative forces behind RIXO, one of fashion's hottest new labels. After meeting at the London College of Fashion, Henrietta, from Cheshire, England, and Orlagh, from near Derry in Ireland, worked as buyers for ASOS, and started their vintage-inspired label in 2015 out of their London flat. Now stocked globally by the likes of Liberty of London and Saks Fifth Avenue in New York, RIXO has a huge following of influencers, fashion editors and celebrities. Henrietta and Orlagh are also multi-award winners, having won the British Fashion Council's Award for International Growth Potential in 2017, Premium Brand of the Year at Drapers Awards in 2018 and the Sunday Times *'Ones to Watch 2020'* in 2019.

Last year, at a Christmas party, we had a bit of a moment. After swaying arm in arm, belting out cheesy songs and laughing at each other forgetting the words, we started swapping our resolutions for the year ahead. To stop constantly striving. To stand back and appreciate the little things. To have more fun. And then it hit us. As friends who are now business partners, the one thing we rarely stand back and celebrate is our friendship. Maybe it was the cocktails or the twinkly lights making us feel all sentimental, but suddenly we were envisaging ourselves at sixty, reminiscing about all the good times we'd had together and kicking ourselves for not appreciating them sooner. So the next day, both slightly nervous and a whole lot curious, we sat down and took this friendship test: fifteen questions designed to remind you and your best friend of all the incredible moments you've shared, the memories you've created, and maybe even reveal a few truths about yourself, too. Dare to join us?

1. Did you honestly like me when we first met?

Orlagh: My first memory of us hanging out is of going for lunch after a lecture and feeling quite relieved that I'd found someone in the class I got on with. Until then, I'd found it quite hard to click with anyone. And before I went to uni I'd taken a foundation course and there was only one girl I'd been friends with there, so I was beginning to think I'd made all my best friends at home. As we were chatting, I remember thinking, 'This could be a potential friend.'

Henrietta: Ha! I actually remember that day so clearly. It was at the start of uni and I was sitting in the lecture hall. You came in late, carrying this gorgeous vintage bag, and I remember thinking, 'She looks really cool, I want to be friends with her!' And then, as luck would have it, you sat next to me! We had a really similar style, and when we chatted later you were super-friendly. I'd also never met anyone from Northern Ireland before, and I loved your accent. So yes, from day one I thought you were really cool!

2. What three things was our friendship first based on for you?

Orlagh: The same sense of humour, an obsession with vintage clothes and charity shops, and pre-drinking vodka, slimline and limes.

Henrietta: 1. A love of vintage and charity shopping. I used to do that with my mum, but no one else at uni was into it. Going to vintage fairs on the weekends was one of the ways we first connected.

2. Our similar attitudes. I'll always remember that university project we did together which involved getting a work placement with a designer. Everyone else seemed to have connections, but we just went round and literally knocked on people's doors. It was probably quite naive, but we both thought, 'Let's go for it' – neither of us felt that was odd or embarrassing.

And 3. Ibiza! And house music. Preferably in Ibiza!

3. What's the one thing you could never forgive me for?

Orlagh: Luckily, it never happened, but after we graduated, when you were seeing that guy who was based in America, I was so worried he was going to lead you astray to live with him abroad and ruin all our plans for the future! I don't bear grudges, but I'd have been so upset.

Henrietta: If you left RIXO, I'd literally be heartbroken. Also, if you moved to another country – actually I don't know if I could forgive that! Even if we weren't living in the same city, I think I'd find it hard. I know we joke with our boyfriends that we have to get houses next door to each other when we get married, but – well, I'm not really joking.

4. What's the best advice I've given you?

Orlagh: How to pack in two seconds flat! I used to fuss for days, laying everything out and stressing about what I should take, but over the years of living with you I've become a lot more laid-back. As you always tell me, if you forget something, just get on with it – there will be shops!

Henrietta: The best advice you've given me is how to do my eyebrows. I remember seeing a mini-toothbrush in your cosmetics bag and wondering what the hell that was for, and you introducing me to brow grooming!

5. What do you think has been *your* biggest influence on *me*?

Orlagh: Perhaps to be less judgemental sometimes? Or a bit more empathetic? I'll always try and look for the good in people, and I think you're better at spotting the bad things. I can be a bit more optimistic and you're a bit more pessimistic. I think both have their strengths.

Henrietta: Maybe to worry less and to go with the flow. I think it's fair to say I'm more laid-back. When we first met, you'd have Saturday night's outfit arranged by Wednesday and your make-up and shoes would be planned in advance – you were always so shocked that it only took me ten minutes to get out the door. You've definitely changed a lot in that way. When I first knew you, there's no way you'd have packed on the morning of flying to New York, like you did last month. I'm proud of you!

6. Can you name one thing you'll never understand about me?

Orlagh: Okay – how you can get ready so quickly in the morning or for a night out! Up and out in ten minutes.

Henrietta: How you lose your keys so often. And your business cards. And your bag . . .

7. How has our relationship changed over the years?

Orlagh: In some ways, it's changed loads – we're no longer students hanging out together, we're business partners – but in all the important ways it hasn't changed at all. We still have a laugh, still go on holidays together, still live together. We're just even closer, everything is out in the open, there are no secrets or mysteries. And our friendship is just as important as RIXO, we always tell each other that.

Henrietta: I think we've become more like sisters than best friends. There's such a huge level of trust. There are friends I couldn't live with, let alone work with. But we live together, work together, go on holiday together – we are together 24/7 and there's never any tension or competition between us. In fact, I can see instinctively when you walk into a room if you're upset. I don't really think of you as just a friend any more, you're more like a sister to me.

8. Which famous friends are we most like?

Orlagh: Ant and Dec, because we do everything together, and we're always finishing each other's sentences!

Henrietta: For a laugh, I'd say Mary-Kate and Ashley's characters in *When in Rome*, having fun together and travelling.

9. Have I ever done something to make you regret being friends with me?

Orlagh: I can't imagine ever regretting being friends with someone. But I think we're both as bad as each other at doing stupid things. Like that time when we did our first ever look-book shoot and got into a car with a random stranger. We heard him chatting in a coffee shop about a building he was squatting in, and both had the same thought – it could be a free shoot location. Next thing, we're heading off in a car to god knows where . . .

Henrietta: I've never regretted being friends with you! But, well, we do seem to get thrown out of a lot of clubs together . . . And there was that university trip to Paris, when we'd all been given a curfew of midnight, but we got in at 2 a.m. I still maintain I'd been saying we should leave earlier! The other students were all in the lobby and they locked the door and refused to let us in. Having to wake up the receptionist, and then the next morning being made to stand up in front of everyone and apologize was mortifying.

10. What's the one thing you can always rely on with me?

Orlagh: That you've always got my back. That reassurance is priceless.

Henrietta: That you're always the first one to give a hug, always the one who wants to clear the air. If me and our other flatmate have had a minor fight about, say, putting out the bins, you're always the one to bring us together.

11. What's your favourite memory of our friendship?

Orlagh: Our month-long road trip from San Francisco to Las Vegas during the university holidays. I think it was our first trip together, and such a fun adventure. We got an upgrade on our hire car and then stayed in these absolute dives. We looked hilarious every time we pulled up at a hostel. The car definitely didn't match the accommodation.

Henrietta: Definitely our graduation holiday, when we took a boat trip around Croatia with a couple of other friends. Swimming in the sea all day, drinking every single night – more of that, please!

12. What do you most admire in me?

Orlagh: Your determination. Especially when reaching out to people on Instagram! And how you take your time to size someone up before letting them into your life. I'm always trying to see the positives, but there have been a few occasions where you've noticed something off about someone before me. You don't let anyone walk all over you, whereas I'm more inclined to try and convince myself things are okay.

Henrietta: I've always admired how thoughtful you are when it comes to buying gifts. You're great at giving random presents if someone is having a rough time – the H pendant you bought me from a vintage fair is one of my favourite things. I love that it matches a little O pendant you always wear, too.

13. When in your life did I really make a difference to you?

Orlagh: I can't pinpoint one time – it's almost every day. I feel like we've been through so many ups and downs that it's an ongoing thing. When I'm feeling really down, or when I'm more stressed and need that extra support, you're always the person who will step in and reassure me.

Henrietta: Definitely during my early twenties. After graduation, when I'd split up with my boyfriend and we set up RIXO. For the first four and a half years we barely went out or socialized or anything, and I think the reason we could be so dedicated was because we were having such a great time together. Since then we've been inseparable.

14. If friendships had superpowers, what would ours be?

Orlagh: I think our friendship almost *does* have a superpower – telepathy! Over the years, we've become so in synch – we can almost read each other's thoughts without even saying anything. I love the fact that when we first meet people, or a new situation arises, we don't need to discuss it in too much detail. We often both get the same vibe.

Henrietta: For me, it's that if I'm ever upset, you make me feel better. And hopefully, vice versa. I guess I first realized this when we were in our early twenties, both working hard to establish ourselves at work. I'd stopped going to the gym, had put on weight and my skin was breaking out – I'd stopped caring about myself, basically. Looking back, I was so self-critical, talking myself down all the time. Out of all my friends, you were always the one to lift me up and give me a strong talking-to if I said something negative about myself. There's a reason I call you Oprah! If one of our friends is struggling, I'll say, 'Talk to Oprah!' We all know that, after a pep talk from you, we'll feel so much better.

15. What's something you've never told me before?

Orlagh: I don't think I ever told you how I honestly felt about the possibility of you moving abroad with that boyfriend. You hinted at doing it a few times, but I was always careful not to say how much the idea worried me. I didn't want to stop you, but I really, really didn't want you to go.

Henrietta: That I literally wouldn't be living in London if it wasn't for you and our friendship. I used to love travelling, so if we hadn't become so close, I would probably be living abroad, maybe in Australia, by now. I guess what I want to say is that my whole life has changed because of you.

FRIENDSHIP UNFILTERED: THE QUIZ

1. Did you honestly like me when we first met?
2. What three things was our friendship first based on for you?
3. What's the one thing you could never forgive me for?
4. What's the best advice I've given you?
5. What do you think has been *your* biggest influence on *me*?
6. Can you name one thing you'll never understand about me?
7. How has our relationship changed over the years?
8. Which famous friends are we most like?

9. Have I ever done something to make you regret being friends with me?

10. What's the one thing you can always rely on with me?

11. What's your favourite memory of our friendship?

12. What do you most admire in me?

13. When in your life did I really make a difference to you?

14. If friendships had superpowers, what would ours be?

15. What's something you've never told me before?

CATHERINE GRAY

What your heaviest-drinking friend wants you to know

Catherine Gray is an award-winning writer whose debut book, The Unexpected Joy of Being Sober *(2017), became a* Sunday Times *top-ten bestseller within a fortnight of publication. A former magazine journalist, she has worked for* Glamour *and* Cosmopolitan, *written for leading titles, including* Stylist *and the* Daily Telegraph, *and is the author of two follow-up books,* The Unexpected Joy of Being Single *(2018) and* The Unexpected Joy of the Ordinary *(2019). She lives in Brighton in a rented flat where everything dates back to the seventies but you can just about see the sea.*

Alcohol is often depicted as friendship glue. We give each other coasters saying, 'Let's go get drunk and judge people.' Or cards saying, 'Good friends offer advice. Great friends offer gin.'

Bahaha! Right? Hmmm, not so fast. What the spirited memes and fridge magnets fail to acknowledge is that booze may bond us, but it can also dissolve us s-l-o-w-l-y, splitting us asunder, often over decades of bad drunken behaviour.

I decided to quit in 2013. It was a no-brainer for me, given my drinking, once fluffy and cute, had grown teeth, claws and underworld-fiery eyes. The 'work hard, play hard' me of my mid-twenties had segued into 'cry into a bottle of wine a night – sometimes more' in my late twenties and early thirties.

My heavy drinking did not go unnoticed, and how my friends reacted followed a predictable pattern.

Stage one: 'You're so fun to hang out with!' Bonding, complete.

Stage two: 'Can we please *not* get hammered tonight?' To which I was like, 'Sure', but secretly: 'I don't think so, my little grasshopper.' I would then 'onemorebar' them into staying out two hours later than they desired. (The epic hangovers which ensued led to friends turning my name into a verb – 'I got Cathed last night' instead of 'I got smashed.')

Stage three was when people started looking at me askance and wondering if they liked me after all.

Stage four was utter exasperation. Friendship fades to grey and, eventually, black.

If you love a friend who's a wreckhead (and I say that with utter love, given I was one for twenty-one years), you may well recognize these stages. I'm sorry. But I'm sorry for your friend too. Since they, most likely, equal or outweigh your sense of exasperation with fear and feel as if they're stuck on some macabre merry-go-round that gets darker with each orbit.

So, I'm here to tell you what your friend is probably going through, in the hope these insights will provoke compassion, spark 'Aha, that's why they . . . ' realizations and, ultimately, promote acceptance. Because however much you care for your friend, the only person who can make them change is – them.

1. THEY'RE NOT REALLY A FREELOADER

I was labelled 'useless with money' by dozens of friends. It wasn't unusual for my card to be declined when it was my round, or for embittered squabbles to break out when I couldn't pay for my portion of the taxi. But my fiscal fuckwittery was not a symptom of my character; it was an offshoot of my addiction.

In my late twenties, I hated being alone (because I didn't like myself, frankly) so I mostly barrelled straight from my work at a magazine to 'a couple of drinks'. Five nights a week. I spent all of my spare cash on tankards of cider, entry to sticky-floored nightclubs and fried chicken, like the 2010, Balham-based answer to Henry VIII. My 'unit diary' revealed that at this point, my most sober week consisted of three bottles of wine. 'You were my big-night-out friend,' said my mate Kate, after I quit. 'I just didn't realize you were everyone's big-night-out friend.'

Now that I don't drink, I'm always in the black; I pay bills early and I try to pay for *more* than my share, if anything. Similarly, I'll bet your friend is not deliberately freeloading. They're just permanently skint. That doesn't mean you *have to* pay for them all night, though. 'Oh well, soda water with fresh lime is free!' is an entirely permitted reaction. (They'll hard side-eye you in response. But that's not your problem.)

2. THEY'RE AN INCORRIGIBLE FLIRT, BUT NOT FOR THE REASON YOU THINK

I've recently discovered that the reason a very close friendship of mine ended was because she'd grown concerned that I couldn't be trusted around her boyfriend. Opening scene: house party, 1 a.m., winter, mulled wine around the fire. Her boyfriend, having mulled himself a touch too far, is lying on the floor in the foetal position. I get down beside him and try to spoon him, because 'he looks sad'. Friend tells me to get the hell up and get my hands off her fiancé.

I remember this. I know I was genuinely not attempting to feel him up in front of her plus twelve of our friends. But I also know how it appeared. And that I would react the same way.

IT'S PROBABLY A PECULIAR BLEND OF FRUSTRATING AND COMFORTING TO KNOW THIS: YOU ARE UTTERLY POWERLESS OVER YOUR FRIEND'S DRINKING. NOTHING YOU CAN SAY, OR DO, CAN STOP IT.

Here's why I was a little handsy when tipsy, a smidge suggestive, a lot flirty: I was the walking definition of 'Daddy issues'. I was a love addict, as well as hopelessly addicted to alcohol. I thought I had to prance around like a show pony to gain approval. I thought people fancying me meant I was a worthwhile human being, and my hunger for validation was as keen as my thirst for wine. I never crossed *that* line with a friend's partner, but I can see why they made damn-straight sure I was never alone with them.

So if you're in that place, too, I get it. Noticing how they act flirtatiously around *everyone*, not just your partner, may make you feel better. Chronic insecurity often manifests itself as Jessica Rabbit-esque behaviour. Knowing what's driving it may ignite some compassion.

3. THEY FEEL LIKE 'FUN BOBBY' WHEN SOBER

Have you seen the *Friends* episode with 'Fun Bobby'? Monica is dating a tall drink o' water who the Friends nickname 'Fun Bobby', as he not only brings *joie de vivre* to the party, Bobby *is* the party. Only, Bobby then quits drinking, having realized he is addicted, and starts moping around like a fun-hoover. 'Fun Bobby' is then dubbed 'Ridiculously Dull Bobby'. For some time (only about, oh, two decades), I was haunted by 'Fun Bobby'. I laboured under the misconception that sober people, especially Sober Me, were terribly, terrifically dull. If somebody told me they weren't drinking, I was a shot-pushing bell-end.

Why? Because underneath my bravado was a cellular-deep fear that Sober Me had zero to offer, socially. That people wouldn't like me. I started drinking very early (your friend probably did too – those who start drinking before the age of fifteen are four times more likely to become hooked). Aged just twelve, I decided that it lit up my drab, anxious personality, just as feeding a coin into a slot machine sets it dinging, whirring and flashing. I was terrified of who I would be without it. This misapprehension kept me drinking for many, many years. I wish more people had told me – as they now have – that the truth was the polar opposite: people actually preferred me when I was sober. (It's not the worst idea in the world to tell your friend this, very gently, if it's true.)

4. THEY WERE A NO-SHOW AT YOUR BIRTHDAY BECAUSE . . .

I called in sick frequently when I was drinking. I alienated colleagues, but also friends, swerving many Big Events you ought-not-miss-if-you're-a-decent-friend: birthdays, engagement dinners, christenings.

I felt hangdog guilty every-damn-time for lying, but in a way, I was telling a partial truth. I may not have been vomiting because of a 'dodgy prawn curry', but I was vomiting. I may not have had flu, but I was experiencing the full-body micro-shiver of it. *I was ill* – it was just self-induced via Sauvignon Blanc, menthol cigarettes and a 3 a.m. finish at Be At One. I know that flash of 'not again' irritation that pulses through you when your friend texts to cancel and you know full well that their reasons are poppycock. I know, I know, I know. But you don't know what scary predicament they have woken up in. Their hands may be shaking, their head pounding, their stomach roiling; they don't know if they can pull off an Oscar-winning performance of a normal person tonight. They might have spent all their money, they might have woken up in a different city, they might currently be at an STD clinic because they can't remember if they used a condom.

The punishment of their hangover – and the ensuing guilt of cancelling – most likely transcends your irritation.

5. THEY'RE SCARED AS HELL

No matter how blasé they appear, they're scared. By their own drinking. By their phone the morning after, which they pick up with the ginger hands of a person handling a pinless grenade. They're scared of the lost hours, and what they did, and what they said, and of losing you. Which is why they will often drop you a 'Wow, last night was off the hook, no? I woke up inside a McDonald's bag' sort of text the day after. Meanwhile, you're livid about the way they behaved. They *know* they crossed a line last night, but they can't quite look it in the eye. The invisible subtext of this chirpy missive is this: 'I've woken up scared. Are we OK?'

Whatever you think about them the morning after, the one thing I know for sure is this: they're thinking a whole lot worse. But they can't reveal the depths of their self-loathing, the reservoirs of worry about their drinking, the sharpied-out hours they don't recall, in case you suggest the un-bloody-thinkable.

That they try *not drinking*.

6. SOMETIMES WALKING AWAY IS THE KINDEST THING YOU CAN DO

Actually, your friend probably doesn't want you to know this. But if they ever quit, they would likely time-travel back and give you permission to bounce.

In 2011, my best friend took me out for the night (paying, as usual) and tried to break up with me, because of my drinking. 'Why is that *all people see* when they look at me?' I wailed. 'If you want people to see something different,' she said, with a weary mixture of grace and grit, 'show them something different.'

Half an hour later, when I yet again tried to convince her to go to one more bar, she threw her arms up, said, 'I can't do this any more,' and left. I dealt with it the only way I knew how: by going to buy another bottle and crying into it, pondering how unloved I felt.

My best friend retracted the break-up within twenty-four hours but was mysteriously ever-busy for the next six months. I later found out she was giving herself a 'secret break'. It's a miracle I didn't lose her altogether. In retrospect, that night was an important smack upside-a-the head; one of hundreds of tiny rock bottoms that led to my quitting.

But I've since been put in the same position myself. Where, after many years of unreasonable behaviour from a dangerously hard-drinking friend, I chose to walk. Which seems brutal and off-brand, given my message of bottomless compassion for addicted drinkers, and maybe even hypocritical, given I've been there myself. But, as much as I love her, I don't like her any more. (Many friends have said the same about pre-quitting me.)

It's entirely possible that said friend will quit one day, and we will then reconcile, but for now, I've chosen myself above her. My own wellbeing, above limping on in a friendship I have to fake. And it's possible you should, too, if you can no longer even *see* the end of your tether, let alone shimmy back up it.

7. IF THEY ASK FOR HELP, GIVE IT, BUT DETACH FROM THE OUTCOME

Five years ago, the same friend told me she knew she had an issue with alcohol and asked me for help. I bought her books, offered to take her to a meeting, sent her links: everything I could think of. Nothing worked.

Of course it didn't, because she wasn't ready. The only person who can help her is her. She was just trying to outsource the quitting to me. Just as I had done myself, so many times. 'Help me!' can sometimes be code for 'Do it for me!'

It was only once I was willing to step up to the plate, throw as much energy into my quitting as I had my partying, and to own responsibility for my behaviour, that sobriety finally clicked for me.

In the meantime, it's probably a peculiar blend of frustrating and comforting to know this: you are utterly powerless over your friend's drinking. Nothing you can say, or do, can stop it.

But if your friend does quit, whether for a month or for ever, this is your time to shine. What was once a shut window is now ajar. Confide in them about the times your drinking has scared you too. Support them in their non-drinking, even if you feel somewhat forlorn about losing your drinking buddy. If they've decided to quit altogether, the likelihood is they've been attempting moderate drinking for years. And spectacularly failing at it.

'That was you trying to moderate?!' said one friend, in utter disbelief. Yes, really, that was me trying to moderate.

The vast majority of my friends tried to talk me back into drinking – 'You're not that bad, just take a few months off!' The few who really got it, who remembered my soberversary, who gifted me Quit-Lit books, who planned gigs and theatre, rather than asking me to watch them drink in pubs that smelled like feet – well, they were the golden ones.